THE OBSIDIAN TRIALS

Seven Spiritual Steps
For
Overcoming Fear

Pamela Santi Meunier, M.A.

Galactica Press

ISBN 0-9669095-0-X
Cover Design by Patrick J. Falso
Cover Painting by Pamela Santi Meunier
Printed in the United States of America

The Meaning Of
The Obsidian Trials

Gazing upon a polished orb of the obsidian stone, you may at first see only black. But within moments, if you look deeper, you will be amazed to see the glow of a mysterious light emanating from deep within the blackness.

I have named this book after the obsidian stone because of this quality of light within dark, and for the lessons in self-discovery that the stone offers us. In mythology, the black obsidian is known as the master teacher in understanding the color black - the absence of light - and darkness. The darkness is our own personal struggle with fear, misunderstanding, and illusion. The black obsidian symbolizes the darkness within each of us, and how that darkness can lead to our self-destruction if we do not see beyond it to that inner light of true understanding and spiritual insight.

Over the last eighteen years, I have been on just such a journey of struggle and self-discovery. My personal journey consisted of seven trials, or lessons, involving my relationship to fear and illusion. Each trial I encountered contained its own lesson and challenge. I have discovered that these lessons are universal in nature and can benefit others, so I have documented my experiences with the seven obsidian trials as a guide.

As a psychotherapist and teacher, I have had the privilege of seeing these lessons work miracles in other people's lives, just as they have in my own. For those who struggle with addiction, toxic fears, or an inability to trust and enjoy life, answers may be found within these pages. Facing our own personal darkness requires courage and perseverance, but if we are willing to fight for the light of wisdom, freedom, and truth, we are rewarded far beyond our wildest expectations.

*We shall not cease from exploration,
and the end of all our exploring
will be to arrive where we started
and know the place for the first time.*

T.S. Eliot

This book is dedicated to my beloved Ioch,
whose wisdom and love have transformed my life.

Acknowledgements

First and foremost I want to thank my husband,
Christopher Curren for his continued support.
His help, like his love, is beyond measure.
Thank you Chris.

I would also like to thank my dear friend and colleague,
Lois Hartwick for her unswerving faith in me and
in my work and her help on this project.

Special thanks and love also to:
Cindy Bullens
Alma Cravatt
Patricia Elliott
Maya Gay
Elizabeth Haich
Pat Rodegast
Lois Van Cleef
Karen Miller

Contents

Contents

Foreword

"Surely the pages turn very quickly and the message is clearly given. Life will bring you every gift but do not look too carefully at the packaging. There is no escaping the walk on the path to remembering. It can take a month, a year, a lifetime, but it will come about because, you see, you do not come just to problem-solve nor to suffer nor to succeed, whatever that may mean to you. You come to bring the light of your true selves into the darkness of illusion, your human world. That is the purpose. That is the path.

"And where does this light live, you might ask. Inside yourselves, overlaid with historic misconception. Now is this historic misconception of a karmic nature or is it current? Well my dears, everything is current, for there is no moment other than the "now" of eternity. Is past life recall useful? If it is allowed to be and is not given the power to relegate you to living or reliving historic moments for their own purposes.

"Most certainly, you are all given the blessed guidance of angels. None of you walk alone. Let this be the first real test of your powers of faith. Do you believe that? Then you are free to explore your world as the true adventurer that you are. If you do not believe in your eternal safety, then you will be distracted by every sudden sound or rustle of circumstance

along your path.
    "You, dearest Santi, have well chronicled all of this and more. An excellent piece of work."

- Emmanuel

Introduction

There is a thread that runs through a person's life. Day by day it is woven into the fabric of the individual. It may pass unacknowledged, but it is there just the same. This story, my personal story, is about that thread, a thread that I have cursed for its piercing pain, and blessed for its sweet grace. The thread is my relationship with God, and the fits and trials that I have been given as a result of that relationship.

There is nothing more personal to me or more sacred than the spiritual events that I have experienced. That is why it has taken over eighteen years to finally complete this work. Up until now I have lived for the most part a very private life. Only a handful of my closest friends know the details of this story, and even fewer participated in some of the events. To those dear friends who were not included in this book, I send my apologies and thanks for their presence in my life. Like a beautiful necklace made up of variously shaped beads, so is my life and the dear friends that I am grateful to have known along the path. For the purpose of this story, however, I have focused not on the intricacies of the various beads, but simply and specifically on the thread that holds them all together.

The presence of God has surrounded me every moment, every heartbeat of my life. There has not been so much as a single second since my life began that I have not felt this presence. It was there while I was being abused as a child, while I watched my parents drink themselves to death, and even in my darkest hours when alcohol and isolation appeared to be all that life had to offer me. This thread has supported me through great pain, challenged me and forced me to look at the depth of my shortcomings and denials. It has chased me relentlessly as I tried to run away from everything good and loving; when my self-esteem plummeted and I wallowed in self condemnation and hate. In the darkest recesses of my nature and in the highest blessings that I have received, this thread has been there, loving and holding me in its Grace. That unconditional love has taught me to love the unlovable, to forgive the unforgivable, to fight for truth at all cost, and to hold steady in the face of my greatest fears. All that I am, all that I know, and all that I can be is because of this thread.

I am telling this story because I have been guided to tell this story. I have fought quite a battle over the last few years between what I have known and what I was willing to share. The responsibility of knowing what was being asked of me, especially in revealing publicly the experiences that I have had over the last sixteen years, has ignited fears that have shaken my very foundation. The fear that I would be judged, thought of as mad, or a liar, have all loomed large in my consciousness. I can now see that these concerns for what other people might think are really projections on my part of the doubts that I have had to battle with, within myself, about myself. Thankfully, as I become more rooted in the truths that have been taught to me, these inner conflicts are less and less. Through these teachings I have learned not to abandon myself to the fearful rationalizations and justifications of my ego. I have learned to not take the details and the obstacles in my life so seriously. In the beginning of this process, I saw my ego as something to be feared and distrusted and by doing so gave it even more power and control, the very thing that I was trying to correct. Nowadays, I experience my ego rather as a clever little imp that is always up to some form of mischief. I love my ego today, and have learned to value its abilities, while placing strict boundaries on its role in my life. By doing this I am better able to be a responsible member of the human community, while keeping a channel open to the spiritual realms which are such a vital part of my life. Practicing this balance has allowed me to complete this book and to finally tell this story, which I have kept private for so long.

It has taken years for me to get past the fear that the "paranormal" nature of my experiences might be deemed too unbelievable. I have come to accept that it is my job to tell the story, and let the reader draw her or his conclusions. The lessons presented in these pages are valid, whether or not events can be accepted as literally true. I ask only that the reader look past the form to the content of the work. My story is about a wonderful and exciting adventure, but in the truest sense I am a very unimportant part of it. I was chosen to be the vehicle, not the journey.

I have an image in my mind of someone who drives across country to see the Grand Canyon, and in each place along the way taking pictures of the car and not the changing scenery. On her return home, she shared with friends a pile of snapshots of just the car. In this example, I think everyone would agree that this would be very odd, and yet our egos try to do this whenever they get a chance; to make the vehicle more important than the journey. In simple terms, I hope that you will enjoy my story. Take what you value from it and leave the rest.

The events and names of the people and places have remained the same with the exception of two people. I changed their names to protect their privacy. All events have been retold as accurately as possible. In addition to my memory, I was aided by several journals, audio tapes and poems that I wrote while these events were taking place. I do want to say, however, that all these resources were personal and based solely on my point of view and interpretation. Even though my intention was to view these events from a transpersonal perspective, I do not claim that I have always succeeded in doing so. It is my hope that the reader will seek to identify with the lessons and tasks within these trials rather than comparing how I personally had to overcome them.

This book is about the process of transformation. Each step has within it a challenge which, if met successfully, heals an aspect of our perception, allowing us to experience other dimensions of consciousness.

Since time began, people from various cultures and religions have been referring to the evolutionary process of the human being back to its spiritual source. This book is about the teachings that were revealed to me in the Great Pyramid in 1981, while I was in an altered state of consciousness. This experience opened a door within my mind that has remained open since that time. I am in no way implying that this is the only path to transformation, although it has certainly been mine. I invite the reader to share in my journey with the hope that for some it will be a source of help and encouragement.

The initiate is, by definition, a student and a teacher for God. No matter what level we are on, we are continually learning and being challenged by the next level, while serving as a teacher for the level that we have just achieved. In this lifetime, I began my journey at the level which involves the aspects of desire and attachment. Attachment is defined as specialness, where we attach ourselves to that which we believe will make us whole. Codependency in adults stems from such attachments and is one of the major challenges. Addiction and compulsive behavior are the other most prominent symptoms. When we overcome these attachments, the next lesson is before us. It is referred to as the "pit of darkness." Darkness and fear challenge us at this level, and many are catapulted back to the lower degrees, if any aspect of the darkness is not overcome. Confronting our greatest fears as well as a terrible depth of aloneness are also characteristic of this lesson.

My journey takes place primarily in my struggle to overcome and become a teacher of these two lessons. The Obsidian Trials are the seven challenges within the second lesson, of fear and darkness. Each Trial must be overcome before freedom can be accomplished.

Here I would like to clarify something that I altered while writing the book for the purposes of literary style. The term "Obsidian Trials" is a term that I devised. It was not given to me directly from my teacher, Ioch. Ioch did guide me to study the nature and truth in the obsidian stone and therein discover the secrets of the Seven Trials.

Although I have just recently completed my initiation, I am still a student struggling with my lessons and my humanness and I assume this will continue as I walk one step at a time through my days here on earth. Given my history, it is not a surprise to me that my work as a psychotherapist has focused primarily on these challenges. Codependence, child abuse and addiction with an overall focus on disempowerment and low self-esteem have been at the core of most of my clients' pain, and this is true for most of my colleagues as well.

I believe that we are facing a unique time in our history. Never before has there been more peace and abundance, and yet addiction and soul sickness are at an all-time high. How can this be? I believe that the "Obsidian Trials" are challenging large numbers of people all around the world today, and that my experiences, while perhaps more dramatic than many, are nevertheless typical. If this is true, then this is a timely work that can aid the individual as well as the community in understanding and overcoming the obstacles that we are all faced with. The rewards are freedom from compulsive behavior and codependency, and an ever deepening sense of wholeness and self worth. The initiate's perception shifts away from the darkness of the world of problems and into the light of the world of solutions. Things that were previously viewed with fear and/or negativity can then be seen as opportunities to problem solve, to demonstrate healing and growth. The overall feeling of powerlessness gradually shifts to a profound connection with an ultimate power that guides us to the fulfillment of our purpose.

This purpose, or dharma, as the Indians refer to it, is our sole reason for manifesting in human form at a particular point in time. A lifetime is never arbitrary or undirected. We may choose to ignore our higher nature because we are granted self will, but this simply delays our destiny and our joy. It is only in the alignment with our purpose that unconditional love and joy can be truly expressed. The journey, however, can be a lonely one where fear feels like your only companion. I have written this book to serve as a guide for those of you who are facing these enormous challenges. I hope that what I have learned can help to lighten your load and serve as a companion and guide along the way.

At the end of the journey, our pain will be transformed into joy, our anger into love, our woundedness into our greatest gifts, and our souls into brilliant beacons of light. I hope to meet you along the way.

- Santi

Chapter One

Back To The Beginning

Rene Ledeux was tall, dark, handsome and very French. I found myself strangely attracted to him, and at the same time oddly repulsed. It was hard for me to look at him directly. This was not out of shyness, although I could be shy. This was something else, something from somewhere deep within me - call it a passionate panic. We were no more than nodding acquaintances when I was invited to an opening of his latest works, to be held at his Hollywood home. Being an amateur painter myself, my curiosity was aroused, so I invited my girlfriend Bea and off we went. Little did I know what earth-shaking changes would begin in my life as a result of that one simple decision.

As we parked the car and began to walk up to the door, I was struck by a sinking feeling in the pit of my stomach. Was this infatuation or my intuition warning me to run? I didn't run. Through the Spanish-arched front window, I noticed an enormous painting and paused to look at it more closely. I could see seven huge white horses in full gallop with their manes blowing in the sea mist, nostrils flared and full of steam. It was breathtaking and it literally stopped me in my tracks. Out of nowhere I felt an electrical charge at the base of my spine shoot straight up through the top of my head.

Stars actually appeared before my eyes and the next thing I knew, Bea was tugging at my arm asking me if I was okay. This was not my typical reaction to new art work, however impressive, and I wondered what was wrong with me. Feeling awkward and strangely embarrassed, I dismissed it, took a deep breath and walked inside.

The room was packed with young, beautiful, southern California artist types, all of whom were much more interested in each other and where the mirrors were than in the paintings displayed around them. I pushed my way through the crowd to the dining room. Cocking my head and balancing on one foot to see over peoples' heads, I caught a glimpse of another picture, one that would change the course of my life. It was a painting of a huge meeting room filled with oddly dressed people from an ancient civilization, and for reasons that I could not explain at the time, I knew that I had been there.

Why did I feel that I knew this place and where was it? I decided to ask my host. As I turned to look for him in the crowd, I was startled to find him standing directly in front of me. He welcomed me with a warm smile and a gracious greeting. So why did I feel like running? Observing my interest, he explained that these paintings detailed the glory of ancient Atlantis in the days before its final destruction. They were set designs for a film of that period that he was working on, and he was selling the originals to raise money for the project.

I felt positively mesmerized by these ancient scenes and was startled by my reaction. The more that I looked, the more I began to "see" myself in those places, not like a photograph, but as if in a movie. An odd sense of familiarity overtook me. Details and faces emerged along with vivid sounds, smells and memories. I remembered having such "flashbacks" as a young girl, but that had been years ago. I couldn't stop the cascading images that filtered through my mind, and I didn't want to. The sense of beauty and happiness that they brought was positively hypnotic.

Rene stood there without saying a word. Did he know what I saw? Did he know who I truly was and that we had been there together in that time? My mind was split between two times and places. Part of me was at the party while the other was in ancient Atlantis, feeling as I did then and possessing a wisdom beyond that which my 1980 mind possessed. My perception was such that I could see my future and the future of Atlantis in the same instant. Time took a flash to reveal its history. A single second contained a detailed century. How could this be? Yet I knew that I knew, clearly and without a doubt.

I looked at Rene and, without a moment's hesitation, said: "There were no golden bulls carved on the main doors. It may look beautiful and dramatic in your painting, but we did not use animal forms in the temple." He said nothing and looked at me, puzzled and somewhat irked.

The crowd came back into my awareness and I shuddered to think that I had said such a thing. Yet, the doors stood detailed in my mind's eye. I knew that I was right, and I knew that he knew that I was right. He just wasn't sure what to do about it.

Bea appeared out of nowhere, giving me the perfect excuse to mingle. I excused myself, got a soda and began to socialize. There were several people at the party that I knew. They helped me to temporarily forget about Rene and those strange paintings. His eyes would meet mine from time to time throughout the evening, but we did not speak again.

That night I had a waking dream. I know that I was awake because I looked at the clock and it was 3 A.M. Rene's face appeared before me and began to change slowly into an ancient face. He was adorned in gold and his head was very long with sharply chiseled features. It reminded me of a statue of the Egyptian Imhoptep, the chief architect of the pharaoh Zoser of the Third Dynasty, that I had seen in a museum as a little girl...or did the statue remind me of Rene?

I was not sure. I knew that he wanted me to do something. We were communicating telepathically, and it was as clear as any words that I had ever spoken or heard. I knew that he was going to ask me to work on his film. I fell asleep and dreamed of the desert. It was an unsettled sleep where I felt pushed and pulled by anticipation and dread.

The next evening, I went out with a group of friends and my boyfriend Peter, when we ran into Rene. He approached me directly with a big smile and an urgent request to talk. I excused myself from my group and we went off to a quiet corner of the room, Peter watching with disdain. Feeling both shocked and not, I listened as Rene asked me if I would help him write the screenplay for his movie, just as he had in my dream. He had heard positive reports of my work as a script doctor on a few film projects and he thought that I would be perfect for the job. Being French, he needed help with the language. Translating was slow and frustrating for him. Was I interested? A voice inside of me started to say, "This is the hand of destiny. It has nothing to do with your being French or my being a script writer. There is a story here that has to be told and only we can tell it."

I said none of that. Instead, I gave a positive, professional response and arranged a meeting for the next day to negotiate a contract. My hope was that I could do this part time, and keep my current job at the production company. I had spent the last few years learning a lot about the film industry and I was moving up quickly. I knew that I would be a producer soon and this project would be a positive step for my career.

Peter was very displeased that Rene and I would be working together. He felt that Rene was evil, and that I was not equipped to deal with such a man. His words scared me, but I felt unable to stop the flow of events that had been set into motion. I felt as though destiny had taken over and I would have to ride it out to its conclusion.

Rene and I arranged to work for a few hours every

evening so as not to interfere with my other job.

The writing went well. There was a surprising ease and clarity to it, an odd sense of <u>retelling</u> the story rather than creating it. At the time, I was so thrilled to be working on a feature film that I didn't question too deeply the source of my intuitive knowledge of Atlantis. I was feeling more and more fulfilled, but Peter was becoming more and more irritable. I could hardly blame him. I spent every night working and devoted little time to our relationship. He wanted to know what was really going on. Yet how could I explain it to him when I didn't understand it myself? It was true that I was somewhat attracted to Rene and financially invested in the project, although those elements were secondary in my mind. What really mattered to me was that I was being driven to do this by a relentless inner call that would take me all the way to the end of the tale. I was powerless to stop it. In the light of this call, all other considerations seemed to dim; my love for Peter, my job at the production company and my friends' concern for my welfare. My mind was unreachable and everyone around me began to recognize this. Peter was losing me and we both knew it. Perhaps I was lost to him the moment I saw the Atlantean painting of the great room with the golden bulls on the enormous door. Those doors unlocked a corridor in my mind that intimately connected me to a past life thousands of years earlier, but strangely more significant than the current one that I was living.

In just a few weeks, we finished the first draft of the screenplay and Rene began to take it around for financial backing. Reaction to the script was positive, but it became apparent that we would need a scientific consultant to validate the material. If we were writing a serious historical film on the fall of Atlantis, it would take more than just our "inner feelings."

Rene called the Association for Research and Enlightenment (A.R.E.) in Virginia Beach. It was the most logical place to start because its founder, Edgar Cayce (the famous "sleeping prophet"), had given thousands of readings on Atlantis, all of which had been transcribed and catalogued in the Foundation's library. Scholars and historians on predynastic Egypt and Atlantis found Cayce's readings an invaluable resource. Rene was already familiar with the material. I, on the other hand, had a lot of catching up to do. As fate would have it, Edgarton Sykes, a world authority on Atlantis, currently was visiting the foundation from his native England to set up a donation of his six-hundred book library. Now that he was in his eighties, he felt that the A.R.E. could make better use of his life's work than he could.

Rene and I decided that this was the opportunity of a lifetime and we were not going to miss it. I quit my job at the production company and we flew off to Virginia to meet and study with Edgarton at the Foundation. This decision was not met with wild enthusiasm by the people in my life. On the contrary, no one was happy about it. My employers were furious with me, and my relationship with Peter was one breath away from the end. I left, willing to pay the consequences, whatever they might be.

We were greeted warmly by Hugh Lynn Cayce (Edgar Cayce's son and the current A.R.E president) and the others at the Foundation. It felt as if they had been waiting for us: long lost friends, finally returning home. It was an extraordinary and magical time. Never before had I been exposed to so many people who were psychically gifted and personally committed to the pursuit of spiritual truth. There was no fanfare; only a desire to know and serve the truth. "A search for God," they called it. I joined their study groups and was delighted to find a wealth of useful information and spiritual support.

I hadn't felt those feelings since I was a little girl, growing up with my mother at our home on the Rhode Island coast. My mother and I had been very close and very much alike in the years before her alcoholism swallowed her up like a tidal wave that destroyed everything in its path. We were both psychically gifted. I grew up assuming that everyone else was equally so, until I went to school, where I was ridiculed for my belief in myself, God, past lives and my "angels". I knew then that I was different and that these things were better kept to myself. After I watched my mother slowly lose her mind from alcoholism, I buried my inner gifts, hiding them from others and even from myself. I did not want to "see" what others did not see, nor to "hear" what others did not hear. It did not feel like a gift, but more like a curse. It had driven my mother insane. Was I crazy too? I lived in fear of that, for there were so many things that I experienced that were unexplainable. Still, I believed that if my heart was with God, my mind could be divinely directed.

Edgarton Sykes was exactly as I had pictured him. He was very English, tall and striking, with a full head of rich, wavy, snow-white hair. He always wore the same old sweater with holes in the elbows, even on a warm summer day. He smelled of old wool and musty books, and I felt as if I had always known him. He agreed to read our screenplay and to tell us if it was historically accurate. If it was, he would be the film's consultant. What a coup! We crossed our fingers and prayed that our intuitions and insights on Atlantis were in fact historically correct.

We had been invited to a dinner party at Hugh Lynn Cayce's house that evening and were looking forward to meeting more members of the A.R.E. Up until this time, Rene and I had been focused on writing and researching the script along with settling our differences of opinions as to "the way things were." Before getting ready for the dinner party, Rene suggested a walk along the beach.

The soft white sand beneath our feet was still warm from the heat of the day. We sat down gazing at the coral sky, listening to the waves lap upon the shore. He took my hand and leaned over, as if to give me a kiss. I felt a deep flush of passion. I was filled with powerful feelings of love. It was all that I could see. How could this happen in one short moment? As his body came over me, it shadowed the sky and I could see his face very clearly. Who was this man? Again, I saw him as he had been long ago. His skin was brown and smooth, his face was long and angular. His eyes penetrated my being, and I knew that he would take me.

We went back to the hotel and made love. As we kissed I felt a change taking place in my body. I was leaving, in a sense, my present day womanly body of a 5-foot, nine-inch brunette and becoming a young girl, petite and delicate. I summoned up the courage to open my eyes to see if what I was sensing was, in fact, happening. It was. But not only to me; Rene had been transformed also. We were making love, but with different bodies, as different people. Suddenly I had thick, long, raven black hair that reflected indigo in the candlelight. My youthful skin had never been touched before, except by the women who bathed me. I was losing my virginity to this man. For a few moments afterwards, as we lay in each other's arms, I was still this young girl as he stroked my hair. Slowly our present-day bodies reemerged. I wondered if Rene, too, had seen us change. I wondered, but dared not speak of it. We showered and went to the party as if nothing had happened. Rene was calm and charming; I was on the edge of panic. If I didn't consciously breathe, I would explode with fear. But what was I afraid of?

*   *   *   *   *   *   *

Alma worked at the A.R.E., converting all of Edgar Cayce's work into Braille. She was a warm and loving woman. I felt as if we had been sisters in a school or convent of some kind a long, long time ago. There was a deep wisdom in her light blue eyes. We spoke very little the first couple of weeks that I was there. I was afraid to share these visions for which I had been so humiliated in school. If I were crazy and kept quiet about it, maybe no one would find out and I could get by. If I were not crazy and these things were really happening, how would I even begin to explain it? Rene was the last person that I wanted to share this with. Even though he was the most logical person, I felt extremely guarded around him. I felt that somehow Alma understood what was happening, but I was not yet ready to approach her. I knew that once I opened up, there would be no turning back.

In the meantime, Edgarton Sykes, having read and reviewed our script carefully, agreed to work on the film as our consultant. He felt the information in our story was accurate, and he was fascinated by how vividly we detailed everyday life in Atlantis. He shared with us the fact that over the last thirty years many film makers had approached him, but until now he had not read such an accurate accounting of Atlantis' final days. And none of those films were ever made. Something always happened to sabotage the process. In almost a whisper Sykes said, "The power and wisdom of the Atlanteans' culture will not be revealed until the world is ready to receive this sacred knowledge with honor. In the wrong hands only more destruction will follow. Be aware that if the time is not right, your story will not be told." Then he smiled, patted me on the back and said, "Let's get to work."

I continued with my research in the library, working with Edgarton on all the details, and trying my best to avoid Rene. I was running five miles a day and doing at least an hour of yoga morning and night, trying to remain in the present and stay in this body. Rene gave me wide berth, but still I felt stalked. What was he up to? He began having long meetings with Alma, and I sensed the quickening of time. I was not going to be able to hide from what was happening. The momentum was picking up steadily, day by day.

Nightly, I dreamt of the Great Pyramid, Cheops, in Giza. I flew high above it or soared up and out from the capstone. I recalled as a child writing the word "Egypt" over and over again to help me sleep on nights when my parents had been drinking and fighting. It soothed me. These dreams had the same effect, like a cool cloth on a fevered brow.

Rene and I shared a hotel suite. Even though a living room separated our bedrooms, I felt smothered. I couldn't breathe. I began sleeping propped up in a seated position to take the pressure off my chest. He hadn't done anything. Why didn't I trust him? He began to shower me with very expensive gifts - Cartier jewelry, designer clothes. He wanted me to look like a queen. Within me the battle of passion and panic continued, and he was becoming more and more impatient. And then, a very strange thing happened.

Rene and I were having breakfast at the hotel as we did every morning. As we discussed the plans for the day, and how the work with Edgarton was going, suddenly, a very striking, buxom woman in her mid-fifties came up to me at the table. She took my arm firmly and looked me straight in the eye. Her gaze went right through me. Referring to Rene, she said, "Be careful! He will do it again if you let him." She stormed away, as if she were angry at his presence. My heart sank. This stranger had spoken what I feared. I was in danger; still my facade remained cool. I laughed off what the woman had said, hoping the sound of my heartbeat would not be heard over the clamor of breakfast dishes and chatter. My inner voice spoke to me, "If you abandon me now, you will surely be lost." It was time to go and see Alma.

Knowing that there was no going back, I walked up the hill to her office. Once I opened up to her and told her all that I had been going through, I would be balancing on a very thin limb. My heart said that I could trust Alma, but my guts churned with doubt. I heard her humming to herself behind her closed office door. As I lifted my hand to knock, she called out, "Come on in." The doorknob was cool under my sweaty palm.

Alma and I were opposite in appearance. She had very pale English skin and light, thin hair. I was freckled and brown, but we had the same eyes. My eyes have been a constant thread woven through my many lives. When I meet "an old friend," the reunion is always in the eyes. We saw and knew one another. She had been waiting for me. I had nothing to fear from Alma.

She handed me a red book, "Initiation" by Elisabeth Haich. On the cover was a picture of a falcon with a strange crown on its head. Alma explained that the bird represented Horus, of Egyptian mythology, the creative principle which crosses space and creates worlds. His crown represented the Ten Commandments, a way of being in the world. I found myself drawn into the eye, the eye of Horus. The phrase was hauntingly familiar. The eye of Horus in "The Book of The Dead" (Chapter 42) states: "I am one who is with the Sound Eye; even when closed I am in its protection." According to the myth, the eye of the moon was lost in a battle against Seth and then recovered. It was this eye that, when presented to his father Osiris, helped him attain new life. Would this book help me attain a new life?

Alma told me to read the book very carefully before I went on my trip to Egypt.

Egypt? But I was not going to Egypt. Alma smiled and repeated her instructions. I thought to myself: I have been here working in Virginia for months; I live in Los Angeles; my relationship is on the rocks; I have made love with another man from another lifetime. Now I'm supposedly going to Egypt. Perplexed, I kept silent and took the book, walking away more confused than when I had come. The value of my meeting with Alma was that I finally knew that I wasn't crazy. Life was not as it appeared. It was filled with crazy, unexplainable things, but my visions were being validated. I felt more grounded, but not on the Earth.

That evening Rene and I attended "A Search For God" study group. The discussion topic was "The Destiny of the Soul" from Book 2 of "A Search For God," and I was struck by a particular passage:

> The development of our souls in a material world
> is as a garment that is made up of warp and woof

of materials that we have gathered through our experiences in every plane of consciousness. In our sojourns on the earth, we wear many kinds of garments - working clothes, prison garbs, and wedding gowns. Just so we build into our souls, through our mind and directed by our will, that which is Godlike and uplifting, or selfish and degrading. That which we build without our soul gives it the opportunity for occupying a position of honor or dishonor. Through the will, however, we may make those things that are of dishonor as stepping stones to positions of honor. This, too, makes its mark on the soul. Our will is a Divine attribute; how we use it determines our destiny.

(p.63 based on Edgar Cayce Readings
262-73--262-90)

What were the marks on my soul? Was I here, now, in this place, for honor or dishonor? While I was deep in thought, Rene took my arm and insisted that we had to talk. A chill passed through me. We were going to speak of an ancient time, a time still unresolved. It gnawed at us both, although we had never spoken of it. Tonight we would.

It was a beautiful, warm September evening. Post-poning the inevitable, I suggested a swim in the hotel pool. Once we were poolside, however, Rene decided to just wait and watch me. As I swam laps, I could feel his eyes on me. Again, the sexual warmth accompanied by an unexplainable repulsion arose in me. Out of breath, I turned onto my back and began to float. I looked over at Rene. He smiled at me seductively. I felt that if I let him, he would swallow me up like a hungry tiger. I knew in my mind that there was no more stalling. It was time to talk.

No sooner did this realization dawn, than my head began to buzz, traveling at the speed of light, propelling me backwards in time. Suddenly I was in ancient Egypt, floating in one of the palace pools. The pool was filled with white and yellow lilies, fragrantly filling the warm evening air. Again, the coral sky surrounded my view and the transformed Rene stood there as he did now, staring at me. My mind became lost in the memory.

Never had a man stared at me in such a way before. I was a virgin, already vowed in the initiate school. I was filled with fear and a strange excitement. I hated the way he looked at me, but at the same time, I felt the power in it. He was draped in fine linen. By his gold jewelry, I knew that he was someone very important here in our new home.

He suddenly spoke. "Is a beautiful flower to be hidden behind closed doors or displayed at the center of a fine table?"

In my trainings at school, I received instruction in silence. So, of course, I did not reply. My face felt flushed. I looked away. Telepathically I heard his thoughts: "I will have this Atlantean jewel. She will be my finest possession."

Swimming to the far end of the pool, I grabbed my robe and ran into the palace, never looking back.

My ears began to ring and once again I felt myself speeding through a time tunnel. In an instant I was back at the hotel pool in Virginia Beach. Rene was holding out my robe. The chilly evening fog had begun to roll in. I dried myself and we sat down to talk as the final sweep of color left the sky. He looked into my eyes, speaking softly but firmly, his French accent caressing each word. I felt glued to the chair.

"Alma said you came to see her today. She and I have been talking for weeks now. I needed her to help me to try to understand what was going on with you. You came here to Virginia to write this film. We made love. It was very intense. I felt that it was also for you. But you have avoided me ever since. You spend all of your time doing research and confirming the information with Edgarton. I know that is why we came here, but what about what happened between us? You haven't even looked in my direction in weeks. I don't know how you feel about me or Peter. I don't know how you feel about anything. So I went to talk to Alma. I somehow knew that she could help me to understand what is going on. So much is happening here. Not just between us but with the film. Everything. Finally, yesterday she told me what it was all about. The pieces fell together. I could feel the truth and the power of her words resonate throughout my body."

He then began to speak of a time that I had been reliving in fragmented visions for the past few weeks. It was now going to be pieced together. He continued. "She told me a story that takes place thousands of years ago. It is a story involving you and me. This film that we are writing on Atlantis is but a small piece of our story - our past. Everything that is happening to us today is because of what has happened in the past. We are being given the opportunity to make it right; to heal and transcend our karma as it were. How we proceed, the choices that we make, will then determine our future - our destiny."

The veins in his neck grew thick and hard. They looked as if they could explode. I wondered about what was going on in his mind as he spoke. I listened silently as he began to tell his tale of ancient Egypt. The battle within me still raged. Part of me wanted to take him in my arms and reassure him that I knew the truth. I didn't need long explanations. My visions confirmed his words. The other part of me, staring at his neck, wondered if he would have a heart attack or a stroke. Why did I silently hope for it? Perhaps then I'd feel safe. Ashamed of these thoughts, I remained silent, showing attentiveness, hiding my disdain and fear.

Rene continued: he had been a high priest (Raji-Amen) in Egypt, which at that time was not only a religious, but a governmental position of power. I had come from Atlantis, a highly developed society, with my father Ptahstepenu (Fa-stefen-u) and a group of fellow initiates from the Sacred

Mystery School. Initiates in the Mystery School were spirited students chosen to dedicate their lives to the sacred teachings that had been brought to them by the Sons of God. These teachings were the Secret Tenets.

My father, part of the Atlantean Hierarchy, was in charge of the care and transport of the Secret Tenets. Four sets of tenets were prepared when the Hierarchy predicted the final earthquake and sinking of Atlantis. These four sets were to be stored in four safe locations on the earth; Yucatan, England, Egypt and the area near present day Bimini. We had been assigned to Egypt, and Raji-Amen (Rene) was in charge of helping us fulfill our mission. My father had negotiated with Raji-Amen for years, although I, being a child, had never met him.

As Rene spoke, visions began flooding my mind. I knew that though this story sounded far-fetched, it was true; I was seeing and remembering it. My heart ached as he talked of my father. I missed him and my eyes began to well up with tears. Ptahstepenu was my soul mate. Why, in my great love for him, did I feel such despair? I felt as if I had done something to break his heart. In all the world the last person I would have ever wanted to hurt was him, and yet I knew that I had. How? What had I done?

Rene's voice rose with excitement as he paralleled the past and the present. This film, our budding relationship, meeting Edgarton, the foundation, was all evidence supporting the truth of who we were and what we were to do. The message of the film was that the teachings of Atlantis would rise up again. The advanced knowledge of the Atlanteans was safely buried in several locations on the earth and this information would be found by those reincarnated Atlanteans worthy of this noble mission.

From the time I was a little girl, I have always felt that there was something important that I was here on the earth to do. Was this the urgency, the Call that lived inside my belly, relentlessly pushing me forward?

I knew that the veil of denial which had clouded my eyes had been lifted. I would never be able to pretend, even to myself, that this life was an ordinary one. I had one foot in ancient Egypt and one foot trying to stand in today. This was not going to change. If anything, the memories were taking a firm hold and encompassing my life. I was beginning to realize that my current life was an extension of my Atlantean life and that from this day forward I would deal more with the past than the present. This life was a bridge back to the beginning, back to the Sacred Mystery School and all the lessons that still lived in my heart. I was now willing to allow myself to remember. No longer would I hold back. I was so filled with gratitude for finally understanding that which had been ever present within me. Yet in my relief and joy I was not to see the warnings along the way, the warnings that would lead me to an unfinished lesson. I saw Rene's face and then the Eye of Horus. Was it Nietzsche who said, "If you can survive that which can kill you, it will make you strong?" Was I strong enough for the task ahead? Only time would tell.

Chapter Two

The Journey

Fate again played a role. A research team from the A.R.E. was preparing to go to Egypt. They had secured permission from the Egyptian and French governments to dig beneath the Sphinx. It was believed by certain Cayce followers, based on many of his readings, as well as by many historians, that the Secret Tenets were buried there. This theory corresponded with another of my visions that was revealed to me.

I was watching a grand ceremony in which thousands of people of all different classes were gathered at the Sphinx. It looked very different then than it does today. The Sphinx sat atop a huge columned building with a grand entry resembling the mouth of a lion. (Centuries of sandstorms have today covered all but the Sphinx itself.) There appeared to be hundreds of steps leading up to it and another set of identical steps immediately descending once inside the temple. I stood in awe of this magnificent structure. It represented the heavens, the cosmos, with the Sphinx atop serving as its guardian.

I stood beside Ptahstepenu, both of us wearing white linen robes. His bore a gold triangular apron with a seven pointed star embroidered on it; mine held a winged serpent.

A flash of recognition flooded my consciousness. I did not know the meaning of the symbol, only that it was somehow very important.

Ptahstepenu handed the Secret Tenets, giant recorder crystals locked in a special red and black stone case, to three men. I sensed by the look in their eyes that this was to be their last mission. Once inside the various levels and tunnels of the temple, they would seal themselves in. The secret chamber, where the Tenets would be safely housed, would be their tomb. This was the only way to insure that the Tenets would be safe from theft.

One of the three men was a close friend of ours from the Mystery School. He was tall and golden-haired with the face of a god. As we said our final good-byes to Tenu I felt deep sadness. He was such a bright light to be extinguished so soon like a flash fire. I was not evolved enough to see his mission as purely an honor. I only felt the loss of my dear friend. He had given so much that I wanted to give him a part of myself. I handed him my most prized possessions, three amethyst eggs that had belonged to my mother. She had died giving birth to me. Her love seemed to radiate from these magic stones. I asked Tenu to take them with him to the chamber and place them beside the Tenets. I knew that they would comfort him as he waited for death to come. In my heart a whisper assured me that I would be led back to these stones again. They were one of my soul's possessions. The world cannot separate us from those special gifts for very long.

As Tenu put my stones in his bag, I looked up at Ptahstepenu. He looked surprised that I would part with something so dear to me, but also proud of my gesture. Did he still love and miss my mother? Of course he did. My father loved everyone, even the evil sons of Belial who had driven us from our home. The sons of Belial had no standard of morality. They sought to overthrow Atlantis and seize its power. It was their selfish misuse of the Firestone, a giant radioactive crystal, that preceded the earthquake that destroyed the continent. My father was a great Ptah. Ptahs in Atlantis were chiefs of divinity. He had risen above the desires and fears of the ego. Tenu walked slowly and gallantly up and into the temple. The Sphinx watched the procession from above.

"Will he be all right, father?"

Reassuringly, he smiled. "He will be home amongst the stars before morning."

In my mind's eye I saw the secret chamber located deep within the desert sand. If you draw a line from the right paw of the Sphinx straight down and another at a 45 degree angle away from his heart, at the point where they meet you will find the chamber. A cold chill came over me as I saw the sacred tomb.

I awoke from my dream shivering, unable at first to catch my breath. I did not share this vision with anyone, but it did not leave my mind no matter how hard I tried to push it away.

Rene wanted us to go to Egypt with the Foundation. He believed that we would be instrumental in locating the Secret Tenets. In his vision of our future, we would go on to make our movie and then unearth and teach the ancient wisdom buried for these thousands of years below the Sphinx. This was our destiny - our life's work. Certainly all of my visions pointed to that as true.

The power of his words resonated through me, but underlying the excitement was a whispered warning. I sensed its soft presence, but could not quite hear the words. Perhaps I did not wish to hear. I wanted only to be a part of some great mission.

Rene's eyes were dark and deep, a well of emotion; his stare more intense than ever before. "There is something else," he paused. "Another important piece to this story. Alma said that we had been lovers. We had taken a sacred vow which produced a child. But something happened and the child died before birth. That special soul is asking once again to be born through us - through our love. He has waited thousands of years for us to come together again. It is important for the world that our son finally be born. He is a great healer and has much to do to help this ailing planet."

I was stunned. Was Rene asking me to marry him and have his child? He stood there waiting for my reaction. I didn't love him. Was there something wrong with me? Was I supposed to love him? It certainly seemed that I should. I felt like Dorothy, being twirled around by a tornado and then dropped in Oz. I knew of the Secret Tenets and where they were hidden. I remembered the white cliffs that sharply cut down to the azure sea in Atlantis and I remember standing in the desert after we had arrived in Egypt, homesick and aching to smell the salty mist that surrounded my former home. The sweet sound of the gulls' cry echoed in my mind, but was sadly too far away for my ears to ever hear again.

My own visions confirmed that we had, in fact, been lovers in ancient Egypt, so why did I doubt his words now? I strained to hear the soft reply of my inner voice but I was still not ready for what it had to say. A precise plan is set in time for each one of us. We can align with it and let the flow carry us or we can try to swim against the current. We are free to choose our course, but not our final destination. That is in the hands of our Creator.

The sky opened and we were caught in a downpour. Thunder and lightning filled the horizon. We hurriedly grabbed our things and ran into the hotel. Thoroughly chilled, I took a hot bath. I needed to center myself before I faced Rene. I knew that he was waiting for my answer. Rene had called room service and there was a warm pot of tea waiting when I got out of the bath. His thoughtfulness made me feel safer.

Cautiously I proceeded. "When we were on the beach and you spoke of our destiny, did you mean we should get married and have a baby?" I timidly waited for his reply.

Rene broke into a wide smile and took me in his arms, pulling me close. "Well, of course that's what I meant. It will be wonderful!"

His smile filled the room, and he kissed me without noticing that I did not share his enthusiasm. He was not waiting for me to answer. 'Yes' or 'no' was not even a consideration. This was meant to happen. Rene believed that to go against it would be to go against God. My ears began to ring again. Later, I would understand that the ringing served as a warning just as a fog horn steers a ship away from a rocky, deadly shore. I excused myself from Rene, saying that I needed some time to assimilate everything. He was understanding. Now that it was all out in the open, he believed there was no way for the plan to fail. Even though Alma had told him that I had the gift of psychic-sight and could see that previous lifetime as vividly as the present one, he was not aware that my intuition kept steering me away from him. If what he was saying were true, how could this be? My intuition has never been wrong. In the darkness of my room I pondered this contradiction until the morning light summoned me to face the day.

Edgarton was thrilled at the prospect of my going to Egypt. Being there, I could capture more fully the atmosphere and power of this very unique place. "Once you fall under the spell of Egypt you are never free from her again. Even if you never return, she stays with you."

He was very pleased with the writing that I had done on the script and said again how happy he was to be the film's consultant. He was heading back to his home in England after completing the installation of his work in the A.R.E. library. I had come to care very deeply for this wise old man. At our parting, I asked him if he had been an elder in Atlantis; I felt as if I had known him forever.

Edgarton smiled and pinched my chin. "I have no recollections of any past lives, I have enough to fill my mind with just this one."

I looked into his eyes, knowing that he held something back, but I did not pursue it. I trusted his wisdom. We made plans to meet at his home in England on my way back from Cairo for him to review my research and fine-tune it before I returned to Los Angeles. I was happy to have a plan to see him again, but even more astonished that I was actually going to Egypt. The bends in the river keep you from seeing too far ahead.

Everything was happening so quickly. Before I knew it I had a plane ticket to Egypt, but I was unable to get a flight with the A.R.E. group. I hadn't been home in months and I really needed to fly back to Los Angeles to get some things, pay some bills and talk to Peter.

Peter had been offered a job in New York City and was planning to move at the end of the month. He wanted me to go with him. Peter did not understand that this was more than a trip to Egypt and a great opportunity for my career. I had to go. I was called to go. Compelled. He presented me with an ultimatum: either I move to New York with him now or forget about us altogether. I tried to tell him that I was not able to make a choice. The choice had already been made by something much greater than I. He felt that all my "high and mighty" talk was simply a smoke screen to mask my lust and greed. Though I cringed at the thought that he might be right, my heart knew that he was wrong and that he would never understand. I was going.

Peter left for New York without a word. A moving truck came and packed away what had been our home together.

I felt as if my life were spinning out of control. I was riding a tidal wave with no way of getting off. My inner conflict deepened. Part of me felt excited, blessed and more connected with my inner self than had ever been. The other part felt as if I had lost my mind and somehow I had connected with a group of people who had lost theirs, too. Regardless of what the ultimate truth was, I was committed and would go wherever it took me.

The first stop was Cairo, Egypt.

At the last minute, Rene canceled his plans to go with me to Egypt - a bizarre development, considering that it was he who had spearheaded the whole operation. Furthermore, I had been so busy getting the necessary shots and last minute items for the trip that I hadn't had a chance to call Alma. It was strange that I hadn't had a single opportunity to talk to her since Rene had told me the story. I felt that she wanted to talk to me also, but that Rene somehow was keeping us apart. But why? Alma was the main reason that I was going to Egypt. As she handed me the book Initiation, she had said: "Read it before you get to Egypt. It will make it easier for you to understand." Understand? The more information I got, the less I understood any of it.

One other thing that I found very odd: Alma had said that the trip to Egypt would not be what I was expecting, that I would not be there for the reasons that I thought. I kept turning those words over and over again in my mind. I felt an urgency to understand what she had meant. I would call her as soon as I got to Cairo. There was so much I needed to clarify.

The flight from Los Angeles to Egypt was via England. It was long and crowded. The fat man sitting next to me smelled of salami and snored most of the way. I began to read Initiation as soon as we left the ground. It was not easy reading. I can usually speed right through a book, but this was going to take the whole twenty-hour flight and maybe longer. As we flew over the North Pole, I saw only ice and snow for hours. I was headed for a great desert where the heat and wind dominated. How strange to see the extremes of life on planet Earth.

On the plane, I made friends with a woman who worked for a prestigious bank in London and made regular trips to Cairo. She suggested that we share a cab, since the hotel was an hour's drive from the airport. I was delighted. We arrived in Cairo at 9 P.M. Just before the plane touched down, I spotted a shooting star. The second one that I had seen during the flight. I made a wish and a promise to God that whatever His Will was for me, I would do it. There was nothing more important. Seeing the Big Dipper in the sky made me feel closer to home. The world is large and I was ten thousand miles from everything familiar. This adventure had carried me far, but the dark sky held the same moon that has comforted me in lonely evenings throughout my life.

The airport was a madhouse of activity and noise. Cairo is said to be the noisiest city in the world. The airport was surely proof. It was hard to even hear yourself think. I was grabbed by some officials with bayonets and led to a desk near the luggage pick-up. I could not understand all that they said, but the bottom line was they did not have my luggage. I was so grateful that I had made contact with Wendy, the woman on the plane. She helped me fill out the necessary 'lost luggage' paperwork. A friend from her office unexpectedly had come to pick her up so I was able to ride with them to my hotel. We were staying only a few miles from one another.

Losing my luggage really shook me up. The chaos and the automatic weapons were all very unsettling. There had been a young Moslem priest on the plane. His eyes were an endless brown. We had not spoken, but had glanced at each other a number of times. My shyness prevented anything more. He wore black robes and an embroidered head scarf. I spotted him from across the crowded airport as Wendy and I were leaving. His eyes met mine and he spoke to me for the first time, "The distance that one travels is not the journey. The journey is in remembering." With a whisper of his robe he disappeared into the crowd.

Cairo is a city of contrasts. No visible middle class, only the very rich and the very poor. Wendy pointed out the magnificent Mohammed Ali Moslem, a large gold-domed building rising up like a phoenix from the filth and rubble of a city that appears to be crumbling underfoot. The pyramids still stand after thousands of years, while the buildings built only thirty years ago are falling apart. Everywhere are buildings with no windows, the plaster walls covered with bullet holes, bombed-out cars decaying in front of them. In 1980, there was still no peace treaty with Israel at that point and tension was high. All public meetings had been canceled due to bomb threats. The Iranian hostage crisis was worsening daily. Would the hostages be released before Christmas as everyone had hoped? It was late September and no relief was in sight. The presidential election held more importance than the lives of those innocent people.

What had happened to my beautiful Egypt? It was filled with violence, poverty and massive overcrowding. This great and golden land that had long ago been my home was very different now, alien and frightening. Where once there had been a sacred hierarchy, now there were beggars, bandits, oil barons and fanatics. My heart ached to see her like this.

Much to my relief, the old hotel was exotic and beautiful and my bed was a welcome sight. I was too tired to be upset about my missing luggage, which contained all of my clothing and toiletries. I would worry about that tomorrow. Tonight I would dream of ancient days gone by. It had been a long time since I had last slept at the foot of the Great Pyramid. I would visit it first thing in the morning.

I was awakened at 4 A.M. by one of the most beautiful sounds I had ever heard. I got up and went out onto my balcony. The night was completely black and only a few distant tent fires sparkled. Out of the blackness sounded a thousand voices chanting their morning prayers to Allah. Moslems pray five times a day and this one welcomed the new day. Hearing these voices but seeing no one was eerie and yet inspiring. I wept as they sang their praises to God. I realized how silent I had been in my relationship with God. I rarely spoke of God. Was I ashamed to let anyone know my beliefs? Perhaps I was ashamed of how cynical many people are of such a relationship. I would forget about them and let the sound wash over me. I felt my fears and cares dissolve like water swirling down a sink. I went back to bed and fell into a deep, long and peaceful sleep.

When I awoke, it was almost noon. My internal clock was still on Los Angeles time. I was dying of thirst so I dressed quickly to go to the dining room. I ordered a large bottle of seltzer and a coffee. The coffee was thick and strong, the kind you can stand your spoon up in. I think I ended up with more sugar than coffee in the cup just so I could get it down. Halfway through my meal, a waiter slowly began to open the linen drapes. The sun had passed around and away from the main window. And there it was: my beloved Cheops, the Great Pyramid, majestically and silently surveying the massive desert. It was much more than I had expected. Mesmerized, I went to the window, not caring what anyone thought. Here was my old friend, truly a sight for sore eyes. Our reunion had begun.

I was anxious to get outside and my luggage was still nowhere to be seen, so I bought a caftan in the gift shop and headed for the Giza plateau. It was quite a hike but I didn't want to miss a thing. Next time I would take a cab. Halfway up the hill was a children's respiratory hospital. There was sand and dust everywhere and not a screen nor any glass at any of the windows. Despite its dilapidated appearance, I was drawn and decided I would stop there on my way back.

The desert was hotter than anything I had ever experienced. Already it was over a hundred degrees and was just past noon. The caftan turned out to be the perfect attire so in that sense I was prepared, but I was not prepared for the energy that I was experiencing from the pyramids. As I approached the plateau, my heart began pounding and skipping beats and I felt as though I were having a heart attack. I sat down on the sand to catch my breath and was immediately surrounded by young, toothless men anxious to find an American wife. Nothing I did seemed to deter them. I soon realized that I was not going to be able to get anything done unless I found a guide or bodyguard to keep these desperate young men away. Finding a suitable person who didn't have similar intentions took some doing. Finally I thought to call Wendy at the bank and she was able to recommend a happily married cab driver named Ameil. He spoke Italian, Egyptian and English, had a pleasant personality and best of all he loved his wife and children. He knew his way around Cairo and the surrounding areas and seemed honest. He was to stay with me throughout my trip and share in my adventure. We became great friends.

That settled, I called the neighboring hotel where the group from the Cayce Foundation was staying. A cold, sinking horror filled my stomach as I listened to the hotel registrar inform me that they had left to return to the United States early. Hugh Lynn Cayce had fallen ill and there had been bomb threats, especially in places where Americans stayed or did business. The A.R.E. group had decided to abandon the excavation and get out while the airport was still open. I almost fainted. I felt utterly alone and ill-equipped to handle all that was happening; the hostage crisis, the military presence, the lost luggage, and now, abandoned. When my parents died when I was a teenager, I had been left alone in the wake of their alcoholism. I had to postpone my grief in order to deal with a mountain of debt and dysfunction. Had I come half way around the world to be lost and left alone again?

My fears subsided momentarily when I received an invitation to meet Wendy for dinner at the Hotel Mena, the grandest hotel in Cairo. I was shocked when armed guards searched and interrogated me before allowing entrance. It was, however, common practice because of all the bombing in any public place, regardless of how elegant. I had been trying to call the United States for days but to no avail. I hoped that if I could contact Rene or Alma maybe I could get some advice, some guidance. I was becoming very scared and the situation continued to deteriorate.

Every day for a week I went to the American Embassy trying to get an appointment. Because of the Iranian situation, in which a group of Americans had been taken hostage in Teheran, many Americans were afraid to travel out of Egypt. I still had received no word about my luggage. Ameil said that this was often done to American writers and if I wanted it back, I would have to buy it back with bribes to the guards at the airport. I had only what I wore and carried on the plane, plus the caftan. I had no cosmetics or toiletries, nor was I able to buy any anywhere in Cairo. Soap and water and salt for my teeth were going to have to do for now. I bought a few more caftans and some comfortable sandals. I discovered that if I covered my head and face with a scarf I was not bothered by the young Egyptian men looking to go to America. In fact, because I am so tall it was assumed that I was a man. My disguise gave me mobility when I was not with Ameil.

I had never been in a position of such total isolation and powerlessness and my fear was barely manageable. I could not get my luggage. I could not get into the Embassy. I could not call home. I could not even buy a toothbrush. All that I had with me were my tape recorder, camera and a few spiritual books and journals. There was only one thing to do. Pray. My inner voice spoke softly and simply: "Use what God has given you. Get out of yourself and help others. This will bring you peace."

Get out of myself? How? Then I remembered the children's hospital on the way up to the plateau. I immediately put on my scarf and headed up the hill.

I was not prepared for the conditions that I found inside the hospital. It was like going back to the turn of the century. The halls were poorly lit and the paint was peeling from the walls and ceilings. In the kitchen, meals were prepared over a large fire pit in the center; the pots and pans were encrusted in black from constant use on a direct flame. The operating room was the worst. A single overhead light shone on old metal tables that dated to the thirties. There was a chipped porcelain basin where the hand instruments were sterilized. My immediate reaction was to pray that I didn't get sick or hurt while I was in Egypt if this was the level of sanitation at a hospital.

However upsetting the hospital's condition had been, the children's ward was unbearable. Most of the children spoke English but were so weak and fragile that our conversations were cut short. Finally I just sat there with them, holding their little hands, their big, black eyes filled with the knowledge of their own mortality. They were so sweet and courageous. I felt very blessed to have met them. After several hours I walked back to the hotel, so grateful for my life, even with all its hardships. At least I had a chance.

After that day I decided to focus on the sick and needy children. I began to travel all over Cairo, sometimes with Ameil, sometimes alone. I visited many orphanages. Most of them were run by the Catholic nuns from Rome. Ameil was a great help with the language. Though there was little I could do to help, I wanted to be able to give the children something when I went to visit. At my hotel I bought all the chewing gum they had in the gift shop. The children happily took the gum, but most of them had to resort to sucking rather than chewing it. They had very few or no teeth, not from tooth decay, but from malnutrition. It didn't spoil their joy, but my heart was heavy trying to mask my sadness. The experience jolted me into an awareness of the things that I had taken for granted, and how little I had appreciated the abundance that we enjoy in America. I thanked God for the richness of my life.

I was interested in visiting Old Cairo, but Ameil was against it. "There is no law there," he said. "No one from the outside goes there. It is filled with disease, cholera and hepatitis. The poverty is beyond anything you can imagine."

He refused to take me there, but I had to go. I didn't want to go. I had to go. I knew deep down inside of me that

I would not be harmed. I was being prepared. I was in an initiation. Elisabeth Haich's book came to mind. She had spoken of walking through our greatest fears, past the appearances, to the truth, a walk propelled by trust. This was my test of trust. All that mattered was that I place my trust in God and do as directed.

The cab driver let me off on the outskirts of the old city and I began my descent into an unforgettable world where centuries fell away with each step. In the turning of a corner I felt myself being lifted to a higher level of consciousness and perception. I was there but I was not there. It was as if my higher self, a pure white light, was the one walking through this place, sharing and spreading light. Observing from a protected place inside of me, I saw a small child no more than two years old drinking from a foul-smelling mud puddle where an animal was defecating. No one appeared to be around, so I picked her up. I was shocked to feel no life force in her little body. It was like holding a rag doll. I had never felt anything like it and the pain of it went right to my core. Her eyes were almost hollow, showing no wonder, no curiosity. Only a small flicker of light remained, and I knew this child would die very soon. I just held her close, not trying to change or fix what was happening. Then my inner voice began to speak.

"Just be present with love and respect for what is happening, don't judge it and don't run from it. That is what is being asked of you. Do not try to play God or to curse God when life appears to be cruel and painful. Simply honor the moment by being fully present for whomever and whatever is put before you."

After a while, an older brother or friend came out into the street and took the child out of my arms and disappeared around a corner. In those few moments I loved that little girl more than anyone else in the world. My love for her lifted me up out of the pain. Is it possible to feel that way about everyone? If love is a choice and not just an emotion, then perhaps it is. My heart was full and I prayed for her to have a peaceful ending to this life and a joyous return to Heaven.

Back at the hotel I spent many hours in meditation asking for guidance to find that fearless place within me so that I could be of service to God. I thought about what had happened to me since arriving in Cairo: the group that I had traveled 10,000 miles to meet and work with had left without me; my luggage and all of my belongings had been taken away and there was still no word about them. Egypt was in turmoil because of the hostage crisis in Lebanon and the still unsettled peace treaty. There was no air traffic out of the country because of bomb threats, so I couldn't leave even if I wanted to. No phone calls were getting through to the United States. There was no apparent way for me to change any of it. I was cut off and alone and I finally accepted that this was the way it was meant to be. I had felt comfort and joy in visiting all the children and I was grateful for the opportunity, but I knew that it was not the only reason that I was here.

In my stillness, the Great Pyramid, Cheops, came to mind. I had purposely chosen this hotel so that I could be close to it, and yet I had by now traveled everywhere from Luxor 30 miles to the south, with its green banks embracing the Temple of Karnak, to the deep, dark tombs of the Valley of the Kings where King Tut was laid to rest amongst his riches. Why had I not yet gone inside the very place that has held my heart since childhood, when I first saw it with the Sphinx in a children's picture book?

I was about to find out.

Chapter Three

Lost Time Remembered

I awoke to the sounds of the pre-dawn prayers echoing in the darkness. From the balcony of my room I watched as the sun came up, showering the Great Pyramid with golden light. I knew in my heart that this was going to be a special day. After breakfast I met Ameil and we headed up to the Gisa Plateau. As we approached the entrance to the Great Pyramid my heart began to race, pounding as if it would burst. My breath was short and shallow and I became acutely aware of my claustrophobia. The entrance was narrow with a sharp decline downward about thirty feet. There was room for only one person at a time. A spindly wooden ladder was used for the descent. As I entered the doorway, I felt a cool, damp breeze on my face travel up the shaft from below. Like the flick of a light switch, suddenly everything went black. When I opened my eyes I was lying on the ground just outside the door, Ameil fanning my face with his newspaper.

"Are you all right? You passed out. I almost didn't catch you." His concerned look was comforting.

By now a small crowd had gathered and I felt very self-conscious. I smiled and with a nervous giggle answered that I was fine. I stood up brushing the fine sand from my clothes and took a long drink of water from the jug Ameil carried with him. It helped to clear my head. I summoned my courage and attempted once again to enter the tomb. Blackness fell sharply and swiftly like the blade of the guillotine. Once again I found myself on the ground, an instant replay of what had happened only moments earlier. I had never fainted before and was confused as to why. The sun was still low in the sky so I knew it wasn't from sunstroke. It felt like a vault slammed shut in my consciousness each time I tried to enter the doorway.

I took a few moments to sit off to the side and quietly be with Ameil. He was worried and felt I should go back to the hotel to rest. I knew that there was nothing wrong with me. In many ways I had never felt better. I was determined to enter my beloved Cheops, to break through whatever held me back.

Ameil suggested he go first to lead the way. We had been all over Egypt together. In some of the tombs the passageways were long and narrow, sometimes only as big as three square feet. Occasionally I felt somewhat claustrophobic, but nothing like this. Seeing Ameil in front of me on the ladder temporarily made me feel everything would be all right. I took a deep breath, said a prayer and started to enter Cheops for the third time.

At that moment the sun rose to a point directly before the Great Pyramid. The light reflected downward like a giant diamond. The blinding flash pierced my mind at the point of the third eye. The light became an explosion of clarity, as if I had been looking through a veil which I did not know existed until it was lifted. I looked at Ameil, smiling and reassuring him. This time I was ready to go inside.

He started down the old wooden ladder. My mind likened this tunnel to a birth canal, opening onto a new world - a new way of living. I gave Ameil the thumbs up, turned and grabbed the first rung of the ladder. Just as my foot searched for the next step, my ears began to buzz and ring at a deafening volume. Blackness descended once again and in what seemed like the far distance, I heard Ameil scream. I had a brief sense of falling and then nothingness. I was in a void which appeared to be moving rapidly forward. I felt no fear, no concern, only a quiet sense of rightness, as if on some level I knew what was happening. I felt overwhelmed by an explosion of emotions that I could not identify. My eyes filled with tears and as I brushed them away my vision cleared. I was standing on the banks of the Nile. It was a different time and I was a different person.

I was a petite, young woman with raven black hair thick as a horse's mane. We had just arried from Atlantis. Hundreds of boats filled with all our possessions were unloaded onto the arid banks of our new home. As darkness fell the sand glowed from bonfires which were lit upon our arrival. I stood for hours on a high plateau watching the men carry our belongings up the hill. I thought of my beautiful green home we had been forced to leave and that would soon be far beneath the sea. When my mother died at my birth I felt a light go out within me. I cried at the loss of this light and at the dark hole it left in its place. Only my father's arms, sweet, strong Ptahstepenu, could comfort me.

I stood alone, looking down on the activity and chaos, and cried again. Another light had been extinguished: the light of my home, the home that the Sons of Gods had chosen for the Children of the Law of One. The Sons of God descended from Sirius, another solar system's star. They came to live in physical form among the sons of men who inhabited the earth. Their mission was to teach the sons of men the nature of the spirit and the glory of the Light known as God.

My father and mother were Children of the Law of One because they were direct descendants of the Sons of God. Their genetic structure and nervous systems differed from that of human beings. When my mother died I came immediately into line to be my father's wife. My destiny was to complete the teachings of the Mystery School by my fourteenth birthday. Then, in the fiery pit of my death initiation, I was to rise up in rebirth. I was to sit at my father's side as a hierophant, to rule the sons of men and teach of divine consciousness and the secrets of nature.

There were ten such leaders in Atlantis. My father was the mighty one who ruled over Poseidon, the largest and most powerful island in Atlantis. Poseidon possessed the giant Firestone, a crystal capable of atomic-like power. Its misuse by the Sons of Belial caused the explosion which ultimately destroyed the continent. The Temple of Iltar housed the Firestone and my brother, its namesake, was its keeper. Five pieces of the giant stone had been salvaged by Iltar and sent along with the five copies of the Secret Tenets to various locations on the Earth. One copy was preserved in the Temple of Iltar, soon to be beneath the sea. Father said that it would rise again, when the sons of men were ready to surrender to the Children of the Law of One and commit to following these sacred teachings here on earth. That event would herald the end of linear time when heaven and earth would no longer exist as separate planes.

We had come to Egypt to bury the Secret Tenets in the heart of the Sphinx in a hidden temple called the Adytum, the Holy of Holies. Once the Tenets were safely in place, father and Iltar would set up the Mystery School. I had only two short years to complete my lessons before taking the sacred throne beside Ptahstepenu. If I were to fail, death would be swift and certain. I did not fear death, but rather being plummeted and reborn into my animal nature, cut off from the awareness of God. If that happened, it would take many lifetimes to pull my soul back up into the light.

Two great Master Teachers, Ioch and Talmus, helped me complete my studies. Talmus was tall and stately with a chiseled face and deep violet eyes. Ioch was round and jolly, mighty in his fearless beliefs but gentle in his approach. Ioch taught me of the love of God, the relationship of the Creator with his children, and the characteristics necessary to overcome the challenges of initiation. He also helped prepare my physical body to receive the Divine Force. I spent my days contemplating God and practicing the Law of One. The Law of One was the First Law in the Mystery School. The challenge for the initiate was to attune the external and internal forces of the material plane. Talmus taught of the Heavens, the secrets of the universe, the laws of nature and the obstacles an initiate must overcome.

One of the major lessons I faced was that of desire and attachment. The initiate must learn to walk freely and joyfully through the challenges of pain, passion, loss and physical fear. As I wept at the loss of my home and my many friends who were scattered across the earth, I knew this was something I had not yet mastered. I felt only loss and sadness. These Egyptians were strange and dark. I feared their customs and the way their black eyes could hide their thoughts. In Atlantis the voice was considered sacred and was used with reverence. Silence was our natural way of being. Daily communication was commonly done telepathically. The noise and chaos of this new land was very unsettling. My weary heart could no longer watch. I returned to the palace where our living and work quarters were being set up.

The blue pool of fragrant water outside my bedroom door looked inviting. I was covered with a typical day's sand and dirt and thought a swim would be a perfect remedy. As the sun set and the moon came up over the rooftop, the coral sky set the sand aglow. My heart opened to its beauty and for the first time since my arrival, I felt at peace. The water, veiled with day lilies, gently caressed my naked, weary body. I floated effortlessly and time seemed to stand still. Suddenly, something began to disturb my peace. I opened my eyes to see what was wrong. At first, the full moon obscured my vision, but then I saw the shadow of a man standing at the pool's far end. His stare made me ashamed of my nakedness. I had never felt this sensation before. He spoke, but I did not allow myself to hear his words. I quickly dressed and ran inside. Father would be expecting me soon for our evening meal. I felt flushed and scattered. I knew Ptahstepenu would sense something was wrong. I resolved to meditate on God until my mind was again quiet. I did not know this at the time, but it was the first of many secrets that I would keep hidden from my beloved father.

Lavender was the color of the inner light that guided me in my meditations and spoke the wisdom of the Sons of God. I chose my lavender robe symbolizing their wisdom. As I approached the dining hall, my inner sense alerted me to the presence of others. My inner eye flashed the dark eyes of the man at the pool and I knew instantly that he was inside. I stared at my lavender robe to gain repose.

Father greeted me warmly as I entered the grand hall. He was excited to have me meet Raji-Amen, his liaison here in Egypt. They had worked together many years to prepare the chamber for the Secret Tenets. At last I would meet this powerful Egyptian priest who was in charge of the Temple of Heaven where the magnificent Sphinx, from above and far below the sacred inner chambers of the Holy of Holies, would guard the Secret Tenets. He served as a diplomat for the Ptahs, priests and pharaohs who held council on the Mysteries. The Temple of Heaven and the Great Pyramid were believed to be located at the heart of mother earth, the most powerful energy point on the planet. It represented the integration of wisdom and love.

Raji-Amen took my hand with a warm, loving smile. Our eyes did not betray recognition as we silently agreed to keep the secret of our earlier meeting. The touch of his hand flushed my face again, but another more bewildering sensation caused me to leave the hall before our meal. A warm trickle began to make its way down my leg. Horrified, I ran to my nursemaid, Keti. I told her that at the touch of Raji-Amen's hand I began to bleed. I feared he was a keeper of the black magic and that my father might be in danger. Keti shook her head and smiled with reassurance. I did not understand. Keti explained that I had crossed the bridge and had now become a woman. But I did not want to be a woman. This body was a cumbersome thing and I yearned to be free of it. I went to bed crying. In one single day, I had lost my home and my girlhood. I felt time moving rapidly, like riding a giant wave with the great God of the Ocean, Poseidon, leading the way.

Weeks passed and we began to settle in. Father and Iltar were busy preparing for the Secret Tenet ceremony. I was being fitted for a gold lapis crown to be worn as a symbol of unity between the Children of the Law of One and the Egyptian hierarchy. My lessons were going well, but my mind was not only on God. Ioch encouraged me to explore this new home.

I had left many dear friends behind in Atlantis. We fellow initiates could talk for hours about alchemy, astronomy, geometry and the meaning of this physical life. Now there was no one to talk to now. I felt very alone. Even Talmus was busy setting up the school. I had so many questions, so many changes happening in my body and my emotional system. Keti was dear, but not able to understand the awarenesses of an initiate. Ioch, who spoke of my aloneness as a means for learning self-reliance and the illusion of separation, said:

> From that point of truly releasing the belief that you are alone, the Sons of God, many of whom are in spiritual form, unite in an eternal bond around you. As your consciousness expands, they become more visible, until the truth can be heard as clear as any robin's song. Then you become part of a circle of love that can protect you from all adversity as long as you never lose sight of it. No initiate can survive the pit of death, the dark night of the soul which is your next challenge, without assistance from the fourth dimen-

sion. Desire and illusion will not take hold if one stays mindful of this truth.

I was afraid. Since my first encounter with this dry, lifeless land, I felt myself changing. I was out of control and hiding it under a facade. My waking thoughts were filled with the Temple of Heaven.

I did not desire communion with the hierophants. I wanted to see Raji-Amen. I felt him luring me towards him. He came to me in sleep, speaking of my beauty and light. I knew that physical love was necessary to carry on the race of humankind, but it was not to be a part of this lifetime for me. My father's union was for spiritual service. Our sexual energy would be channeled upward to the third eye where the creative forces could manifest. However, my teachings did not prepare me for the powerful temptation that I felt. Would I lose myself and sink into animal desire, or rise up like the phoenix triumphant? Could the circle really protect me from this fire I felt smoldering within? I would go to the temple and speak to him. Surely Raji-Amen would stop his mind control if he understood my mission. I was to be a hierophant; there was nothing more sacred. He would withdraw his hold and I would again be free to think only of God. I would go after my morning meditation with Ioch.

During our meditation, Ioch silently sent me a warning. He said never to forget this life was not mine but a holy gift that would be taken away if misused. His jolly face grew stern and sharp. I had never seen him like this before. I acknowledged his words but carefully masked the fear they instilled. After prayers I journeyed to the plateau. The Great Pyramid could be seen for some distance, its giant crystal cap spreading rainbows over the sand below. I paused in awe of the great Sphinx atop the temple and prayed:

Oh, magical, mysterious Sphinx, touch my heart,
Caress my soul.
The power and the calm - the strength and the
Serenity.
Surveyor of all time.
History passes as you remain.
The head of a man,
The body of a lion
Symbol of mind over matter.
Mind over all minds, over all forms of matter.
Help me to stay true to the secrets that we will
Place within your heart.
Oh, keeper of the keys, do not lock me out,
And keep my Brothers of Light always around me.

I reached in my apron for my mother's magical amethyst stones. My hands began to pulsate and grow warmer as I held them. A soothing comfort spread up my arms and through my body. I would not let this dark man rob me of my heritage and destiny. I was a descendant of the Sons of God! What morsel could a son of man, high priest or not, possibly offer me?

The steps to the temple were steep and hot underfoot. There he was, standing in the grand entrance, waiting for me. My strength and resolve melted away like candles after a long dinner. What was it that I was to say to him? Why had I come? In that moment I knew that I had come to be with him. He held his hand out to me.

"Come, I have something to show you."

I took his hand. He led me down a long, cool corridor that smelled of musk laced with a sweetness I could not identify. Raji-Amen escorted me deeper and deeper into the heart of the temple until we finally came upon an immense stone door. It was reddish black with a large gold triangle enclosing a seven-pointed star. A white glow emanated from it.

"Come." He began to open the door.

This was the sacred temple of the Holy of Holies in which only Hierophants could enter. They had met in this room for years to build up the energetic forces for the housing of the Secret Tenets. We could not enter this place.

"No," I insisted, "I am not ready."

He laughed at my seriousness, placing his hands on my cheeks and pulling me close. "You are so naive. Do you think that only the high Ptahs are worthy to receive the gifts of this place?"

"I am not speaking of worthiness," I replied. "I am speaking of purity and vibration. Only perfected initiates have a high enough vibration to protect the sanctity of the Secret Tenets."

Raji-Amen pulled me even closer. My heart was racing. "You speak too much for such a little one."

Then he kissed me. The cool corridor filled with heat and time seemed to stand still. Once again he reached for the door. Instantly, I was filled with fear and began to cry.

"Please do not open this door," I pleaded. "Do not take me in there. My friend Tenu has been chosen to be buried here with the Tenets. If I enter I could endanger his afterlife. I am only at the level of desire. Please, I love him dearly. Do not make me go inside."

I sobbed and shook. The thought of hurting Tenu was more than I could bear.

"Hush, you silly child. I wanted to show you this place to honor you, to celebrate our union, not to frighten you. We can go to my chamber if this is not to your liking."

Pulling away, I replied, "I am not here for pleasure. I am here to tell you to leave me alone, to stop invading my dreams and my thoughts. I am not here to live as a woman. You must stop this now!"

His dark eyes drank the whole of my being. I felt swallowed up by a force I could not resist.

Firmly and quietly he spoke. "The destiny of Atlantis is not the destiny of Egypt. You are a visitor in my land. When I saw you I knew we were to be one. Nothing you do or say will divert my intent. I will have you because you are already mine. I could only enter your dreams by your permission. You know that. I am not fooled by the newness of your body. Your wisdom surpasses your years. Do not stoop to playing a sniveling victim. It is not becoming of my queen."

I stood there motionless. His words were true. The lies were to myself and my family. I loved him at first glance as I swam naked in the pool. I was pleased that he had seen the beauty of my body. What was happening to me? I had wanted God all my life. It was all that filled my mind. Now I could not even think of God. This man was everything. My sight was blinded to all else. My fear fell away with ease, like a cloak upon entering a cozy home. Standing straight and tall, I followed him to his chamber. In his arms the lavender light within me ceased. I became a prisoner of the flesh, locked in matter, my soul yearning to fly free, my heart leaden, groping for affection.

Weeks passed swiftly. With the ceremony only a few days away, I successfully hid my secrets from everyone. Even Ptahstepenu did not read the lines of passion written in my mind. It pained me deeply to deceive him, but I felt powerless to stop. A strange part of my mind took control. I was convinced everything that happened was all right, although I was not able to remember why. I could not yet see that by joining with Raji-Amen, I had been catapulted into the deepest, darkest pit of desire that an initiate can withstand. My passion left me visionless, unprepared for the final lesson that was quickly approaching.

The morning before the ceremony, I spotted Tenu meditating in the palace garden. We had barely spoken since arriving in Egypt. He spent most of his time in silent rites of purification. Although he was a few years older than I, we had been fellow students in the Mystery School. His eyes were the color of the sea that surrounded our home; his hair like the wheat that filled the fields and valleys. This was his last day on earth. I did not feel the honor of his sacrifice, only the sadness of losing a dear friend. I asked if I could sit with him for a while before my fitting for the ceremonial robes.

Tenu replied, "I have witnessed a change in you, Santi, an attachment to things that are of no importance. You believe that you are losing me as you have lost your home. Atlantis is not lost. Have you forgotten so easily the Law of One which says nothing that is rightfully yours shall ever be lost? We only lose illusion. Truth and Oneness are everlasting and solid, be it ether or flesh. This is not good-bye. We will reunite for the final lesson. Of this I have no doubt."

Tenu finished speaking, exhausted from the outpouring of his much needed energy. His vibration had to be kept at the highest level if he were to successfully enter the sacred chamber and seal off all the entrances to the tomb.

"Tenu," I asked timidly, "If I fail, will I lose you?"

"You cannot fail. If you lose your way, it will only be temporary. I must rest now, Santi."

He closed his eyes and resumed his meditation.

I felt alone with my despair. Tenu did not understand. I had lost contact with my essence, my God. I prayed for a sign, for some reassurance that my love for Raji-Amen was providence and not doom. Suddenly a spectral light flashed across my eyes. The face of a male child flooded my vision and clamored in my ears. Instantly, I knew that I was with child. In horror I ran out of the garden. Tenu, lost in his meditation, did not notice my panicky flight.

I knew nothing of childbearing. How could I know for certain that this was true? Maybe this revelation was born from my fear and not the rightness of the Higher One. I had once overheard Keti speak of a crystal that, when briskly rubbed on a woman's forearm, would turn bright blue if she was with child. I would go immediately to the crystal room.

In my urgency, I did not raise a protective guard to hide my inner thoughts. As I entered the crystal chamber, Iltar was waiting for me. He held a pink translucent stone in his hand.

"Have you come for this?"

I stopped dead in my tracks. Once a fellow Atlantean enters the mind of another, they become one. He knew everything. No secrets were possible now.

"Iltar," I pleaded, "I love him." I could not stop the flood that washed over me. "He loves me too and will marry me when he discovers I am carrying his child."

I grabbed the stone and rubbed my arm. Almost instantly it began to turn blue. There was no doubt.

"No one knows but you. What are you going to do, Iltar?"

"Do not underestimate your elders, Santi. Knowing is not synonymous with action. Action is a decision of the will. Letting go is aligning the will with the knowing. Those who dwell in the fourth dimension allow the will of man its choices. I love you, dear sister, but I fear the path that you are on will lead to darkness."

"Iltar, If you knew of this physical love, maybe then you would understand. I am soaring! Everything is brighter and clearer. How can this be darkness? I will go to him now."

Embracing Iltar, I could feel the tears within his heart. He would be fine as soon as Raji-Amen and I were married. I hurried off to the Temple of Heaven. I felt the eyes of the Sphinx following me as I crossed the plateau. It spoke. "You have left the golden temple of wisdom, little one. Walk cautiously."

There was an unusual amount of activity on the plateau. The ceremony would begin tomorrow. Brightly colored banners and flags were strung everywhere. How would I ever find Raji-Amen in this crowd? I stood in silence for a few moments, trying to gain a sense of where he might be. His private chamber came to mind, so I decided to try there first. Just outside his door, I heard the voice of my father and Raji-

Amen arguing about protocol. But I could not hear more than that. I was afraid to get too close and have father pick up my energy and discover me. I went to Raji-Amen's private library to wait.

His desk was filled with papers of a very sophisticated papyrus, one of which bore the seal of the Sons of Belial, fire-hoofed Golden Bulls. How could this be? They were our enemy. They had destroyed our home and gone on to conquer other lands and peoples. Why would there be a letter from them? My temptation was to read the letter, but to do so would violate his trust. This I could not do. I would ask him directly.

The door sprung open. Raji-Amen stood there, glaring at me. "What are you doing here? I was just with your father. He might have sensed you."

Trying to pacify him, I said, "I know, but I had to see you." I walked towards him for an embrace, and spoke the words I knew would save me. "I am going to have your son. I was in the meditation garden when the image of our child flashed before me. I verified my vision with the fertility crystal."

I put my arms around him. I sensed he was stunned. He remained silent for what seemed like an eternity, and then he spoke: "What do you imagine we will do about this male child of yours?"

Reassuring him, I said, "We will be married, of course. Once the sacred marriage takes place, father will understand. Everyone will understand once they see how much we love each other."

He looked at me with mockery. "You really are naive for one supposedly so wise. Do you think that I would risk my reputation and position at the temple for the love of a woman? Love and passion fade with time; position and power grow if you are vigilant." He paused, nervously twisting the gold chain that hung around his neck. "However, I am in a position to keep you. I have wealth enough for that.

No one would judge me for fancying such a raven-haired beauty. But marriage is out of the question. Of course your family, Santi, was one of the wealthiest in all of Atlantis. Would you retain your inheritance if you did not share the throne with your father?"

He stood there arrogantly, coldly facing me down. I felt my life force drain, as a numbness spread through my body.

My mind was not able to fully comprehend his words. I ran as quickly as possible, not even stopping to see if he had followed until I reached the uppermost part of the plateau. I was out of breath, my mind still reeling from what had just transpired. I looked over at Cheops, the Great Pyramid. We Atlanteans had been building it for years under the precise instructions of the Sons of God. It was to be our House of Light, Knut. Cheops would be used for initiation ceremonies and secret Mystery School practices. The large Firestone crystal piece, brought from Atlantis, was placed as the capstone to generate energy and to serve as a beacon for the Sons of God on their occasional journeys to earth. It was comforting to see Knut.

For a moment I forgot the truth that I would soon have to face. I managed to make my way back to the palace without being seen. Keti took me by surprise. I had forgotten the arrangement for the fitting of my ceremonial robes.

"Little one, you are flushed. Is everything all right?"

Keti's concern was inviting. I desperately wanted to share what had happened, but dared not do so. Keti did not have the gift of discrimination. If I told her, everyone would know. This would have to be kept secret until I found Iltar. He would help me.

"Keti," I said, "the sun has burned my face. I still have not adjusted to this great heat. A bath of aloe after our fitting would be perfect."

Keti never thought to question such a logical explanation. A daughter of humans will always believe that if a thing is logical, it is true and, therefore, of value. The

Children of the Law of One know that truth has only one formula. Truth is eternal and never less than true. It does not fluctuate with circumstance, space or time. It is the heartbeat of God, constant and omniscient.

I had fallen so far from truth I could not fathom how I would retrieve it. As Keti removed my ceremonial robes, I spotted the matching apron. There was something different about this apron. I took it from her. She resisted, and I knew she was trying to keep it from me.

"What is that?" I asked in a sharp, somewhat annoyed tone.

Opening the apron, it revealed a caduceus, a winged staff representing victory over the dark forces. I was not worthy of this apron. I had not gone through the pit of darkness in the belly of the House of Light.

"What is this?" I repeated. "I cannot wear this tomorrow. I am not prepared for the test of darkness. Remove this immediately and bring me my old apron."

"Your father insisted that this be made for you for tomorrow," she said. "Talmus and Ioch have told me you are ready for the journey of liberation. It is to happen after the Secret Tenets are placed in the Temple of Heaven. They wanted to surprise you. The stars are in favor of the journey at this time."

Happily, Keti trotted off, so pleased with the revealing of her secret. Little did she know what it really meant. I knew I had to find Iltar. The initiation would have to be stopped. I could not survive the pit of darkness with its fearsome trials without being purified. I had broken the sacred oath of the Mystery School, which was chastity. The most I could hope for was a lowly position in the temple, but never again would I be redeemed and allowed into the Mystery School. I had failed the test of desire. I had failed Ptahstepenu. He would sit on his holy throne alone. My heart broke at the thought of hurting him. He was pure light and love. How could I face him shrouded in shame?

Keti called to say that my bath had been prepared. As I walked past my clothes, which had been tossed upon the floor in a heap, I saw the corner of an envelope. It could not be, but it was.

It was the letter from the Sons of Belial that had been in Raji-Amen's library. How had it fallen into my garment? My hands became red hot as I held it. To read it would be to break the law of honor, but honor mattered little to me now. I felt that fate had played a hand in this miraculous event. I would not let it pass unrecorded. I opened the letter which began with a warm greeting to Raji-Amen. It spoke of a plot to discredit Ptahstepenu and the Children of the Law of One. It would begin with the seduction of his daughter, Santi, heir to his throne and the supposed suicide of his son, Iltar, in the desert. With both his children gone he would be vulnerable. This is when they would attack and take control of the Temple of Heaven.

My vanity and foolishness cut like a knife within me as I saw the truth of that which I called love. My humiliation was a meaningless spark in comparison to my concern for my beloved father and brother. I had to warn them, but how to proceed? Caution resonated through me. I remembered the words of Ioch. "Step from the center of your being. Only from your center will the path be of wisdom and safety."

I became very still, kneeling before my altar. It featured a small statue of Cheops with the seven-pointed star of Sirius hovering off to the left. This was my mantra for purification and clarity. I meditated for several hours. Images of home floated through my consciousness. Golden green Atlantis, where the bluest of all seas sparkled like diamonds in the morning light and the silver clouds were lined with teachers from a distant star.

I was a candidate, a young initiate of great promise. The test was to recognize and reject all worldly desire and temptation. Completion of this test immediately sends the initiate into the challenges of the pit of darkness; the lessons of fear. To succeed was to fly free of attachment and to serve the world through love and wisdom. To fail was to plunge deeply into the pit of the darkest desires of man. I longed to dwell in the golden room of wisdom where illusions fade and fall like autumn leaves. I had worked so hard yet failed so easily. Now I was chained to my lowest nature. Now we, myself and the child growing within, would pay the price of my failure. I knew that only through the evolution of my soul's responsibility would I once again return to my true mission of service and teaching.

The initiate is taught that Karma is a debt that must be paid. To try and run from one's destiny is absurd. Can a strand of pearls remain a strand without the string that holds them together? There is a divine plan that must be followed, its terms and agreements honored if we are to know peace and true love in this physical form. I recommitted to my God, displaying my failures in front of him as a merchant his wares. I prayed:

> *Angels soar on sturdy wings to heights unknown*
> *To man.*
> *I, confined to fragile limbs until I understand.*
> *God, guide me to the path of reconciliation and*
> *Wisdom.*

The star above my altar began to glow and vibrate. The brightness of the star forced me to close my eyes. As I did, a blinding, white flash struck my forehead at my third eye. In that moment I was filled with pure awareness - complete love and understanding. I knew what I must do. I took a few deep breaths, basking in the warm glow. But time was short and I needed to begin my preparations immediately. I felt the fate of my dear Atlantean brothers and sisters balance delicately in my hands. This time I would not fail.

I summoned Keti to fetch my finest robe and jewels, which were fused with the hypnotic scent of lilac, a sacred scent brought to this planet from the Sons of God. I went to see Raji-Amen. The letter had to be returned to his desk before he noticed it gone. He must not suspect me of having any motives other than love. He had always minimized the power and the gifts that we Atlanteans possess. Let him think of me as a foolish, lovesick girl. This would serve me well. His guard and insight would be down.

Moving from my center, I entered his private quarters. He was in the dining hall with several priests and Pharaohs from different parts of Egypt, gathered here for tomorrow's ceremony. Seizing the opportunity, I swiftly crept down the hall to the library and returned the letter to its original place. I was halfway back down the hall when Raji-Amen's voice shouted, "Halt!" He came out into the hall and saw that it was me. "What are you doing here?" he asked with disgust in his voice. "I hope you have not come here to beg me to marry you. I do not have time for this foolishness."

He turned as if to dismiss me. I kept breathing deeply, trying to stay centered.

"I have wonderful news! Can you pull yourself away for just a few moments?"

He motioned to the men and took me into the adjoining room. "What is this supposed good news?" He was clearly impatient and annoyed.

Smiling and bubbly, I announced, "I have spoken to father and he knows about the child." Of course this was not true, but I knew that they would not have an opportunity to speak until after the ceremonies, and by then it would be too late. "He wants to negotiate. It is true that you have wealth and power here in Egypt, but it cannot compare to the great wealth, wisdom and worldly power of my father as the Ptah. If you agree to marry me, he will let you sit beside him on the sacred throne representing the Children of the Law of One. At the time of his death, we will rule together and our son after us. In a private ceremony tomorrow, he will give you all the jewels and riches of the Queen's chamber in Cheops, including access to the power of the Firestone. You and I will enter the tomb and take our pledge of loyalty. It will be announced to everyone that evening in the Great Hall."

I could see that he was overwhelmed and surprised, but he appeared to believe me. I remained in deep concentration. It was crucial that the shadow of suspicion not shade my brow.

"Why would Ptahstepenu forgo so much of this power?"

I answered quickly. "Because if I am disgraced, it will discredit his whole mission here. The Children of the Law of One will be belittled. He cannot permit this to happen. It is worth much to my father for us to save face. He is offering you more than any Pharaoh now possesses. The condition is that you must decide here and now with me, and that no one must know until the announcement tomorrow night. It is important to Ptahstepenu that this in no way interferes with the ceremony for the Secret Tenets. They must be kept separate, each heralding its own festivity."

I was reading him very carefully. Already he was imagining himself sitting on the throne. I could hear his thoughts plotting my brother's and father's death. I felt the fiery rage growing inside my breast, but my face showed only innocence and love. He took me in his arms in a passionate embrace. His kiss felt as long as a lifetime.

"I never wanted us to part. I really do love you, Santi," he said. "There was just too much as stake. Even now, I am kept here too long. The men will be wondering where I am. Tell your father that my answer is yes. Tell him that I love his daughter and we will make the announcement tomorrow!"

He was filled with passion. Not for me, but for power. Does he not know that the power of the world stays in the world? Only the power of truth and love accompany us to heaven. I looked deeply into his eyes.

"Remember, not a word, my love, until tomorrow." I blew him a kiss and left. If I were not so clear in my resolve I would have felt dirty and ashamed. The thought of his touch, once relished was not despised.

I watched the coral sunrise with Cheops silhouetted in the morning light. I felt a strange fondness for his desert place. I bathed and prepared for the day's events. Ptahstepenu escorted me to the plateau. Iltar had gone up earlier with Tenu and the other men. My father was my toughest challenge. His keen awareness could cut through the shrewdest opponent. He knew me well. I had never tried to block anything from him but this time, I prayed I would succeed. To fail would mean the death of my whole family.

I remembered my lessons in the Mystery School. Ioch would guide my concentration. "Be mindful, Little One. The dance of the heartbeat and the breath is the dance of life. Be in harmony with this dance and your life will flow like the river. Through concentration you can slow the heartbeat and the breath to a point of stillness. This is the stillness of empowerment. Nothing in the universe can penetrate an initiate who has mastered the dance of life." His words comforted me as I stayed focused on my breath and heart. If I did not waver, Ptahstepenu would not discover my plan.

I dressed for the ceremony. The final touch was the lapis and gold crown designed as a symbol of unity for our merging cultures. What a deceit! So many questions plagued my consciousness. Why did the Children of the Law of One allow the Sons of Belial to overrun Atlantis and destroy everything? Why did father not know of Raji-Amen's plot against him? If he did know, why has he done nothing to stop it? Does Ptahstepenu see the destiny that lies before me? I did not understand. I just knew what I must do. My commitment was absolute. Nothing would keep me from it.

The sun was blindingly white, already scorching as it rose steadily in the sky. I closed my eyes and filled my mind with beautiful images of home: the gentle, soothing sounds of waves lapping upon the shore, the taste of salt on my skin and the blanket of fog that would wrap itself around me on my morning walks. I remembered the gulls' cry through the mist, the dolphins' impish laughter and the pearl white cliffs bathed in sunlight. All this would soon cease and painful memories would no longer plague my heart. Peace comes from doing the right thing, no matter what the cost. "Sorrow's jewel." Father's words came to mind:

> *Sorrow is a covering, a mask, an illusion, a container. The turtle has a shell, but it is not a shell. It may seem cumbersome, slowing down its progress along the path, but this is a misperception. No moment, no event, no action is arbitrary. The universe is precise. If we focus on the sorrow and the pain, it expands like oil spilled from its container. Our protective shell thickens as fear reigns, making us harder to penetrate. To find the jewel, an initiate must have more faith in what is unseen than in what is seen. If there is vigilance in this, a commitment to the truth...soon all will be known, and the jewel will sparkle in the light once again.*

I was afraid I loved my father deeply, but I could not see through his eyes, only my own. My sorrow was my battle. No one could fight for me. Was my body merely a covering for the jewel of the child that I could feel growing inside of me? Was he covering for a jewel that lay hidden even deeper within the two of us? Was this physical experience simply a nest of boxes fitted precisely within each other until the jewel of nothingness, the great void, reveals itself on the far side of death?

I heard a rap on my door. It was Father. The time had come and the ceremonies were about to begin. As we walked together in the grand procession, I felt the queen in me float to the surface, the power of my commitment elevated to a state of fearless grace. I knew that I would succeed.

At the bottom of the steps leading up to the Temple of Heaven was a temporary platform adorned with fragrant flowers brought from Atlantis. I snipped a small yellow rose from the elaborate bouquet. These delicate flowers from our homeland would soon die in the scorching desert sun. Tenu, Arnot and Be-An stood guarding the Secret Tenets. Father began to speak, his words eloquent and inspiring:

"The greatness that is the man/Spirit/God will rise up and shine forth again from within our hearts, touching the grateful tears of Heaven's guardians as they welcome us home."

Tenu stood beside me, his gallant energy radiating out into the crowd. I remembered us as children discovering a spiral cave nestled within the cliffs overlooking the sea. It was our private castle where he and I were king and queen, the gulls and egrets our countrymen. Tenu was a golden child, son of my mother's dearest friend Terra, who died in Lemuria shortly after his birth. Our common loss bound us together in friendship. Silently, I spoke to him:

"Tall and golden, shining knight of the light, adorned in silver, racing like the wind. A chariot ablaze in glory. A piece of me goes with you in this parting - perhaps the piece I value most of all. Take my mother's amethyst eggs and place them in the care of the Tenets. The brilliant star that brought us here has much to teach before a reunion is possible. Remember Santi. She will not forget you."

I handed him the eggs while Father looked on with approval. I placed the rose in his robe pouch. "This rose was never meant to live in the desert. Take it home to Sirius." Tears filled my eyes as Tenu turned and walked away. Ptahstepenu loved him as a son and felt proud of his courage. I felt my world fading from sight. Would Father think my sacrifice courageous or an act of will? Maybe I would never know. There was no time for grieving. Cheops lay before me.

The crowds dispersed after the ceremony. Only a select group from the hierarchy was to accompany us to the Great

Pyramid. Talmus and Ioch were waiting for me there at the entrance. Father and Iltar were by my side. Talmus draped the apron over my robe. I handed Iltar the lapis crown. Raji-Amen looked on, lusting for power and riches. Ioch spoke silently of my final instructions.

I turned to my beloved Ptahstepenu for a final embrace. I knew that the moment he touched me he would know of my plan. My only hope was that he would honor our oath of loyalty to never disclose that which is asked to be kept secret. His arms were strong, his energy as clear as a diamond. He spoke silently to me from his heart:

"There is a place above the mist where healers ride on blazing chariots. They journey towards you now. The Circle of Healers will be your guides from this day forward. When the Sphinx is in the sand and the earth trembles from a great explosion, the sand will open up to reveal the sacred chamber. The Secret Tenets will be rediscovered by the Children of the Law of One. I will be in your heart, but will not see you again until then. One last thing, Santi. When next we meet, I will be called David. I will practice medicine. You will remember the squareness of my jaw, the shape of my hands with the healing sign upon them. Good-bye, my dear child. I will not interfere with what you must do, for you were destined to do it."

Ptahstepenu turned and walked away. He never looked back to see me enter the tomb. I summoned to Raji-Amen to take my hand. Iltar and the others looked stunned. I kissed Iltar good-bye.

"Brother dear, do not let the sweet smiles of these Egyptians lure you into the desert. There is only death there for you."

He grabbed my arm, fearing for me. I pulled away, reassuring him that I knew the mission and the price. Father told him to be still. Even far away his inner voice could be heard by us. Raji-Amen smiled as he took my hand and we walked into Cheops, his aides following closely behind. The narrow passageways were long, winding to and fro, leading to the heart of the pyramid where the jewels of Atlantis were stored.   Raji-Amen was anxious to see a piece of the Firestone that was securely sealed in a large stone box. We pushed the heavy stone lid away to reveal one of the most powerful tools of Atlantis. What Raji-Amen did not know was that even this small piece of the Firestone was radioactive and would kill anyone who came into contact with it who was not a purified initiate. Only those who had successfully raised this vibrations would dispel the damaging effects of the stone. Everything has a positive and a negative force, even a healing stone. I knew that Raji-Amen would be dead before he and his men could cart the treasure away. He would have his jewels, but they would be his tomb. Relishing his jewels, he did not even notice as I headed for the initiation chamber, Ioch guiding the way, and both of us knowing what was about to happen.

The chamber was empty except for a stone altar at the center surrounded by candles. Ioch said nothing as he watched me enter, but communicated everything, his eyes deep wells of wisdom penetrating my higher mind. I drank his words.

"Santi, for you death is certain. The challenges of initiation cannot be met with the impurities on your soul. But we will come together again when the seeds of your amends are harvested. Go now and face the fear. Remember, it is not real. It simply delays your destiny. Hold in your mind this truth: that you can never lose what is rightfully yours. You are a child of God, messenger of the Law of One. Nothing can change that. I will always be near."

The stone door was pushed shut and I was sealed inside. I was alone. Each breath grew thinner. The candle flames grew fainter with each moment. Darkness and death drew up its cape to enclose me. I sensed the child within my belly and I knew that I was dying. The pit of darkness, the most fearful of the fearful, was upon me. I was powerless. The essence of my fear shone clear as I felt the life slip from my child. Questions raced through my mind. The world needs the peace and wisdom of the Children of the Law of One. Would Ptahstepenu and Iltar be saved? Would the Sons of God greet me? Tenu, will you be there on the other side? My tomb grew darker as my lungs gasped for air. As I lay on the altar, a cold dampness surrounded me. Each breath felt like my last. My ears began to ring and I felt comforted. An angelic voice spoke lovingly to me:

"You are the fortress, the warrior, the unattached defender of the Law of One. You have fallen, and in the descent risen beyond the power of the sons of men. The barren desert is now a fertile valley sown in wisdom; your stone tomb transformed to feathered wings of freedom."

I heard the gulls cry and smelled the sweet sea air of my home in Atlantis. As I opened my eyes, the Circle of Healers appeared before me. Tears welled up. "I was so afraid that you would not come." One of the giant healers looked at me and smiled. "When you understand that we are always with you, you will never be afraid again. We have come to take you home." I then went off into the light.

Chapter Four

The Pit Of Darkness

Smelling salts jolted me awake, and I saw Ameil standing over me. His look of concern softened as I began to smile. The color slowly began to return to my cheeks and the ringing in my ears subsided. I realized I must have given him quite a scare. I took a long drink of water and then he helped me up and over to the cab. Ameil wanted to take me to a doctor, but I knew that there was nothing medically wrong. As we made our way across the plateau towards the hotel, a wave of sadness came over me. How Giza had changed since long ago and yet, in another sense, stayed the same. Although my eyes gazed upon the world, I did not feel that I was totally integrated with my body. I felt like an observer watching from a distance, having no connection to what I saw. I needed to be alone to process what had just happened. I knew Ameil would not understand. Maybe no one else would. I had been changed and transformed; perhaps I had returned to my original form and purpose. I was led back to the beginning, to trust and embody my true self again. Even the name Pamela, which had been given to me in this lifetime, no longer felt appropriate. I was led past my Pamela personality, beyond the limits of her littleness. I knew that I had come home, and that part of the homecoming was to take ownership of my soul name, Santi. The truth filled my heart and cleared my mind, and I sat down and wrote this poem:

What is in a name--a shallow promise or a
Divine order?
Am I my parents daughter? I think not.
Birth is not ownership--it is permission.
Pamela is a symbol locked in form--cramped.
Too small for the space I now fill.
God created wings so we could soar.
Man cages in order to control.
Santi is written on my Soul,
boundless in its passage through time and space.
It was whispered in the Calling,
my heart forever altered by the sound.
It was there at my first breath,
and will be at my last sigh as the final lesson
is learned.
I am not yours. I am not mine.
On the ashen back of the Phoenix,
I rise up to the boundless bliss of Always, Santi,
my Father's child!

Taking ownership of my name and true purpose gave me the clarity and strength needed to face the task ahead.

Ameil and I arranged to meet the next day to retrieve my luggage. I did not care how dangerous it was or how many bribes I would have to make. I would no longer passively sit back and be treated this way. The urgency was apparent. I had to leave Egypt as soon as possible and break all ties with Rene Ledeux. I knew that no matter what it would take, I had to liberate myself from him. I knew in my heart that if I did not break free, he would do to me again what he had done before. I had to protect myself before it was too late. I had been given a second chance and I could not afford to fail.

My lesson was to overcome all forms of desire. The initiate must pass the tests of temptation through understanding and detachment. All forms of compulsive and addictive behavior are challenged. When the initiate successfully frees him or her self from these challenges, the darkness is then immediately before him or her. The initiate's relationship to fear on all levels leads to the final challenge: walking through the pit of darkness and facing ultimately the darkest fear. If the initiate is successful, he or she will be freed from the desires of the physical world. Fear for one's physical well-being slips away. Physical death is understood as a liberation, something to be embraced but not feared. This liberation enables the initiate to be of selfless service to humanity and to the guides that instruct them from various levels of consciousness.

Once again I was faced with these lessons. I had been seduced by Raji-Amen in Ancient Egypt, and now by Rene Ledeux in this lifetime. If I was to succeed, I knew that I had to let go of him completely. I had to break my film contract with him, no matter what the cost in legal fees and penalties. Leaving the film about Atlantis wrenched my heart, but I had to trust that the project was not what it appeared to be. It held nothing but despair and eventual destruction.

Ioch's words centered me: "Trust only in Eternal Truth, all else, no matter how brightly it glitters, eventually fades and is seen as tattered illusion."

I knew that to break free from Rene would mean to be released from the lesson of desire. Even if it took most of my inheritance, I would extricate myself from him. I was not aware that achieving this lesson would immediately set into motion the lessons in the pit of darkness, and the tests of fear that lay ahead of me. Egypt was not done with me yet. Rene Ledeux held the test of desire, but the bowels of the desert held the pit of terror that I would find myself in before the next day's end.

It was time to retrieve my luggage. In the United States, this is a fairly simple matter, but not during the peace treaty disputes and the hostage crisis in Egypt. Cairo was besieged with bomb threats from various terrorist groups. The airport was enclosed by six rows of metal and barbed wire fencing, all manned by armed guards. The only way through those gates was to possess an airline ticket departing that day. Either that or bribing each group of guards at every gate. The risk for bribery was arrest, but it was one I was willing to take. I needed my luggage and a ticket out of this country so I could get back home and free myself from my associations with Rene and the film. The time was now. I feared if I delayed I would be lost.

Ameil picked me up at the hotel after breakfast. I had cashed a large sum of traveler's checks in medium-sized bills. I hid the money in various places in my clothing. My heart was beating rapidly as we drove to the airport. Every few minutes, Ameil asked if I was sure that I wanted to proceed. I would nod and stare out the window, praying for courage. After about an hour, we arrived at the first gate before which stood a young guard in full combat uniform. He was equipped with bayonet and hand-grenades. Ameil spoke to him briefly in Egyptian. The guard smiled and held his hand out for some money. Ameil took some bills from the stack that I handed him and we were then waved through.

The same procedure took place at all the other gates. I was not yet concerned how much money this would cost. I just wanted to get it over with. We finally made it through all the gates, and I thought to myself that a mountain had been made out of a molehill. This was no big deal.

Then I noticed Ameil was not headed for the airport's entrance. Instead, he had driven around back towards a part of the building that appeared deserted. I asked what he was doing and suddenly I felt afraid. "The guards told me to go to the passageway underneath Gate 3," he said. "Someone should be there to take us to the luggage store room."

This seemed odd, but I hoped the worst was over. We found the passageway, parked the car beside the dilapidated building and waited for the guard who appeared a few moments later. He signaled us to follow, something that under normal circumstances I would never have done. He was unkempt with shifty eyes and a strong smell of tobacco. The passageway was a small narrow corridor, about six and a half feet high, with bare light bulbs hanging from the ceiling about every twenty feet. We were underneath the old airport. The walls were cracked and dirty with bugs skittering in and out of the holes. The guard walked several feet ahead, coughing and spitting. He suddenly turned and made a gesture for some money. Ameil handed him three bills. He held them in his opened hand for a few moments and then we went on. He led us through an intricate, underground maze. By now, we had made so many turns I was not sure we could find our way back out. As we ventured deeper towards the center of the building, the air became more stagnant and foul smelling. It made the slums of New York City appear wholesome. What, I wondered, was I doing in this sewer? Would I ever get out of here alive? I always prided myself as being worldly. Had that pride embroiled me in a situation from which I would not escape?

My heart pounded in my throat. I was sweating from head to toe. I kept looking to Ameil for reassurance, but he looked as scared as I felt. My mind was racing. Had I been set up? Was I being led to my death or rape or both? No one even knew where I was. I had been trying to contact the States for weeks and had never gotten through. The U.S. Embassy in Cairo was so busy I hadn't been able to get an appointment. If I were to die in this awful place, no one would ever find out. Was this how it would all end, to be murdered in a dungeon-like hell-hole? Even if I screamed, I wouldn't be heard over the roar of the plane engines overhead. How could I have been so naive and stupid? My arrogance had once again set me up to be hurt or worse.

I prayed for help. Thankfully, my teacher's voice came into my head. It was Ioch, my master teacher from the ancient Mystery School. The sound of his voice within my mind soothed my fears.

"In the pit of darkness you must learn to trust the truth and not the illusion. If you fall for the illusion the fear will overtake you. There are two forms of death in the physical world: those who appear to be alive but are dead to the higher planes of consciousness; and those who appear to be dead but have formed an allegiance with the being of light in the fourth dimension. If you are focused and 'alive' on the higher planes, nothing will harm you. The very light you shed will turn evil eyes away from you. You will be of no interest to them."

I did not fully understand what Ioch meant, but I repeated his words over and over again: "I am alive on the higher planes, my light will deter them."

We were approaching a corner where a bright light shone onto a hall. Ameil took my arm. His hands were cold and sweaty, but firm. The guard began talking quickly to us. I didn't know what was being said until Ameil asked me for more money. I reached into my left shoe and took the last of my bills out.

"This is all I have left. What is happening?"

The guard grabbed the money and pulled me towards him as if to embrace. His hot breath was repulsive. He looked deeply into my eyes. Ioch's voice once again echoed in my mind. "The light will repel the darkness, summon the light!" I remembered my circle of healers. Silently I called to them for help as I stared straight back at the guard. The circle appeared before me and surrounded the guard. They were visible only to me but the sight of them brought me joy. I began to smile as all fear instantly left me.

The guard looked confused and afraid of my reaction. He let me go quickly and pushed me around the corner. To my relief, I saw directly ahead a large room in which smaller caged rooms were filled with tattered luggage. An obese man sat inside one of the caged rooms, spitting tobacco juice into a tin bucket. His feet were propped against my luggage. It had been cut open and the zippers were broken, but it was there. When I realized we were actually in the baggage pickup room, I was able to inhale my first deep breath of the day. The guard handed the fat man some money, who unlocked his room and pushed my luggage out with his foot. Ameil and I grabbed it, thanked them hurriedly, and without so much as a glance, turned and started back the way we had come. I hoped Ameil had a better sense of direction than I, or we might never get out of there.

The hot desert sun was a welcome sight as we emerged from the belly of the building. We hugged each other and laughed nervously for a few moments to release some of the tension. Then all the energy in my body drained out. Barely speaking, we drove back to the hotel where I collapsed into a deep, long sleep. While I dreamt, the circle of healers appeared before me once again.

"You have succeeded, Little One. This is a long awaited day. You have overcome the first test and have emerged victorious. You may now wear the apron that was made for you so long ago."

Ioch placed the apron over my head and I saw the caduceus symbol.

"The power of this symbol and the knowledge and courage now attained will help carry you through the other trials to complete your initiation."

It had taken many thousands of years to get back to where I had begun. "Thank you, Ioch. I will wear it proudly."

I awoke with tears of joy trickling down my neck. Now I could leave Egypt. The test of freeing myself from Rene, however, awaited me.

Chapter Five

Letting Go

Boarding the plane in Cairo was like finding an oasis in the desert. As I dropped into the seat, I breathed a deep sigh of relief. So much had happened. I found myself loving the old Egypt, feeling strangely more at home there than any-where else in the world, but present-day Egypt was deteriora-ting and frightening. I was happy and relieved to be on a flight headed for England. I planned to make a brief stop to see Edgarton before going back to Los Angeles. I hoped Edgarton would make some sense out of what I had experienced. I needed some validation. A part of me feared this whole experience was a massive hallucination. Maybe I was going insane. What if these voices in my head were simply delusions, and Ioch a mere figment of my imagination? Could it be that Rene was just a typical Holly-wood film producer intent on having a relationship with me, and not the reincarnation of some power hungry high priest seeking retribution? How could I know for sure? My mind was content to spin these fearful scenarios, fueling my insecurities with each possibility. I knew that I had to discipline my mind. I could not afford to have my energy drained in this way. I had to stay centered and still. Only by listening to the wisdom in my heart could I cease the nervous chatter in my head.

The train ride to Brighton was pleasant. The sight and smell of the sea calmed my spirit. I bonded with the ocean from my earliest years, having been born on a small island in New England. The sea nurtured and sustained me through many hardships and had always been my companion. My body felt parched after the dryness of the desert and seemed to soak up the salty spray like a sponge. Walking from the station to Edgarton's house, the charm of Brighton began to calm me. Gulls swarmed around the pier, their cries triggering memories of those ancient times when the valley was green and sea gulls sailed around my home in Atlantis.

Then Ioch's voice filled my mind. "There will be a time of reassurance and rest, Santi, but the trial will not be over until your aloneness fulfills you."

His words made me shudder. I had spent most of my life alone. "Please Ioch," I pleaded, "Let me be a part of something, not always on my own. I already learned how to be alone, having traveled across the globe, supporting and educating myself. Why can't I have a family like everybody else? Is that so much to ask?"

My questions went unanswered. Ioch's words addressed my greatest fear, one that I have run from since childhood: the fear of being totally alone, never really connecting with another human being, never really mattering to anyone. Was this to be my fate? I could not accept that. There had to be another way. As I made my way down the street, my mind pushed Ioch's message away.

My visit with Edgarton was brief, but reassuring. His calm, English reserve was like an anchor to this troubled vessel. I settled down in a house filled with books for a soothing cup of tea and conversation. Although he offered no explanation for what had happened in the Great Pyramid, Edgarton historically substantiated many of the details in my memory. Our visit was over much too soon, and I found myself wishing I had booked a later flight out of Heathrow.

I had a deep affection for Edgarton. I feared this might be the last time I would see him alive. Just before leaving, he remembered wanting to give me a book he had written on the Great Pyramid. He rummaged through the stacks of books piled to the ceiling in his living room. I wondered how he could find anything in this disarray, but to my amazement, he located the small pamphlet with ease.

Serving as a wise and loving teacher he said, "Read this carefully. When you understand the mystery of the Pyramid and its capstone, you will understand the lessons that face you now."

Edgarton was a true gentleman. As I walked away, I could not help but turn for one last look at his kind face surrounded by that silver mane. It was in fact the last time that I would see him.

On the flight back to Los Angeles I was filled with anticipation. Rene was going to meet me at the airport. I had tried to make other arrangements, but he insisted. He was anxious to hear about my adventure, and read my script. He interpreted the cold hesitation in my voice as fatigue. This would not be easy. Attempts to explain would be fool-hardy, and perhaps dangerous. I would just withdraw, simply quit and pay the consequences. I could feel the plane descending. The sinking feeling in my stomach confirmed what I suspected: there was no getting out of it. I would have to confront Rene.

I began to pray, "Help me stay centered in my truth, to follow the Light. Dear Heavenly Father, let me never forget who I am and why I am here even if no one believes me. Let me never doubt the gift of this revelation. Help me to let go of anything that does not serve my purpose here. Show me the way and fill me with courage. Thy will be done, not mine."

The bell rang to fasten our seat belts and moments later we were on the ground.

I didn't know if my legs were rubbery from the long

flight or the fear of facing Rene. I called to Ioch to walk with me and felt his presence at my side. I smiled again at his nearness. Rene stood out in the crowd with his tall, tanned physique. His charisma radiated and the crowd seemed to part in his path. I kept praying as he greeted me with a big smile and a long hug.

"How was your trip? I was so worried about you. I let the A.R.E know you were all right. Hugh Lynn took ill in Cairo. They were lucky to get out before all the mess started."

His questions were endless, and after awhile they all blurred together. My luggage had been boxed because of the damage, so we had to go to a special room to get them. The crowds began to disperse from the baggage area and things quieted down.

"Rene," I said, "We have a lot to talk about, but my head is spinning. Let's wait until we get in the car."

He agreed, not suspecting what I was about to say. The freeway was strangely deserted, and because of the time change, I felt disoriented. Rene suggested we pull off and go to the beach to talk. Sunset over Santa Monica beach was truly beautiful. Even the smog added to the rainbow of color. As we stood on the cliffs looking down at the beachgoers packing up their blankets and paraphernalia, everything that I had been through seemed like a dream. Was there anyone in that crowd that saw the way I saw, or heard the way I heard? If there was, would we recognize each other?

Rene waved his hand in front of my face, "You are a million miles away. Is anything wrong?"

I looked at him and knew there was no more time to delay. "Rene," my heart was pounding and my temples were hot. "I am finished with the film. I will give you my research notes and all the written material, but as of today I am off the project." He tried to interrupt, but I stopped him. "There are no explanations that I can share with you. I have made up my mind, and I will not change it. I am sorry."

At first, he was understandably shocked, but that soon turned to fury.

"What about all our plans, our child that needs to be born? We both stand to make a lot of money on this film. Can you just walk away from that? Where will you walk to? I have you tied up in contracts. You are not in control here, I am. You are mine, the film is mine, and I will not let you go."

"Rene," I said feeling calmly detached, "You can't control me any more. Once you could have, but that was a long time ago."

"I don't know what is going on!" His voice turned shrill. "But I'm going to find out what happened to you in Egypt. Everything was fine. Now you are like a different person. What's changed?"

I did not reply. The silence was as thick as the fog that had begun to roll in from Catalina. He dropped me off at a friend's place where I would be staying until I moved back East. I wished I had the courage to tell him everything, but I did not trust his persuasive powers. I feared he would distort events to fall in his favor, a skill he had carried within him into this lifetime. I believed this was best, to make the break and start over. I told him I would reimburse him for all expenses, and that we would use lawyers to talk about the contract. I knew I didn't have a leg to stand on in that matter, but I hoped I would have enough money left to start over. As it turned out, I had to sell my mother's wedding ring and my Cartier watch for airfare back to New York. The remainder of my money would go for an apartment deposit.

Rene tried to contact me several times before I left, hoping that I would change my mind or at least offer an explanation. I stuck to my resolve, but it took its toll. I was in a weakened state and felt very vulnerable. Forfeiting all my money was a big risk. I had gone from driving a Mercedes and living in a beautiful apartment in the Holly-wood Hills, to sleeping in a friend's guest room and scrounging rides. I had lost everything. Or had I? The strange thing about losing everything is the curious kind of peace it brings. When your worst fears have come to pass, there is nothing left to fear. I had hit bottom, much as I had with my alcohol abuse years earlier, but like then, I was on my way up again. I found something else, a gift I never expected. The less I had on the outside the more richness I began to feel on the inside. I hadn't lost everything. On the contrary, I had found me. I had rediscovered my true self and my sense of purpose. No one could ever take that away. The truth of what happened in Egypt was a healing banner around my heart. My reasons for living began to shift 180 degrees, and a new perception of the world started to dawn in me. In losing everything I had found that which can never be truly lost - my soul's purpose - and that was worth any price. It wouldn't be long, however, before it would be tested again.

Manhattan was a welcome sight. Upon arrival, everything seemed to flow more easily. I found a charming apartment on the upper East Side, a short walk from Central Park. I went to the old film production company for a letter of recommendation. I was taking a big risk because it was the same company that I had quit in Los Angeles to go to the A.R.E with Rene, but much to my surprise they offered me a job. I was all set.

With a job and a home in place I was now ready to face Peter. He was working just a few blocks from my office and I called him to see if we could get together and talk. He still sounded very angry, but agreed to meet me for dinner. I tried to explain what had happened in Egypt, and why Rene was able to have such a hold on me, but he didn't want to hear any of it. He could not forgive me for running off to Egypt or the affair with Rene. He wanted no part of me. I was crushed. I loved him, but I could see that his heart was closed to me. I hoped that time would heal the pain and that he would forgive me.

Months passed and I fell into a routine at work. Gradually, the glamour of the city faded and I yearned for a simpler life in the country. Peter and I would go out, but his anger was a wedge between us. I could hardly blame him. After all, I had left him for another man. He wasn't interested in any of my "far-fetched excuses." I was tired of trying to explain. I wanted to forget about everything that had happened. Egypt, Rene Ledeux, Raji-Amen. What was it all for? All it had done was ruin my life. I had no money to speak of, the man I loved hated me, and even worse, I was beginning to experience a worrisome pain in my lower abdomen. Ioch's voice kept fading with each passing day. Once again I was totally alone. I was used to personal loneliness, but the loneliness of losing my inner teacher was unbearable.

"Ioch," I cried. "Why have you left me alone in this darkness? What have I done wrong? I let go of Rene and the film, and now I feel that you have let go of me. Please, let me hear once again your calm wisdom." No answers came, just an interminable silence. I was in a different kind of desert now, a lifeless desert of despair. The only voice I heard was my own, telling me what a fool I had been.

My sister and I owned a house in Rhode Island that was being sold. I hated to lose our wonderful summer house, but it was too difficult to keep and I was in no position to buy her out. The sale would provide only enough money for a down-payment on my own place in the country. A ray of hope began to shine on the horizon. I knew I had a lot of healing to do, and Manhattan was not the place to do it. My plan was to keep my job in the city and go to the country on week-ends. Peter called to meet for dinner and celebrate the sale of my house. As I described my plans to him, his eyes began to open. I could see he was shifting in his feeling towards me. He had taken the job back East because he too had a similar dream. When I was hired for the film and went off to Egypt, he wrongly assumed that my career was what mattered to me most, and that I would never want to settle down in some small New England town. Now he began to consider he might have been wrong. Suddenly, we had a common goal and vision. It started to bring us closer together. I wondered whether my dreams for a simple life with a husband and children could work out after all.

I had been on my own supporting myself since I was fourteen. My parents had died of alcoholism not long after I graduated from high school. But home life had been very unsettled for many years before that. The saddest part was when I realized that the mother and father I loved disappeared many years before their deaths due to the ravages of their addiction. Their souls had been swallowed up by alcohol and the madness it brings. In truth, I mourned the loss of my parents years before their actual death.

My childhood was a time of pain and abuse, and I wanted no more of that in my life. I had thought a successful career would fill that empty place, and for awhile it appeared to. But time has a way of teaching us about the truth. Maybe time would be on my side now and I could leave the events in Egypt and the mission behind me. Since earliest memory, I felt a strong need to be of service, to live a life based in purpose and meaning. Egypt and the Initiation School filled that need in my heart, but it seemed more than I could handle. I wanted a normal purpose, one that you could take pictures of, place in a photo album and share with a friend. I wanted to be a wife and mother, rather than a missionary for God. Was that so terrible? Ioch would understand, he would not fault me for it. As I pushed my true identity far to the back of my mind, a cold chill went up my spine.

Peter and I began our search for the perfect farm in the country. We looked in Connecticut, but high interest rates and inflated real estate prices drove us further and further north. Berkshire County in the southwest corner of Massa-chusetts, seemed like the perfect spot. I had never been to that area. The Berkshire Hills were covered with snow, and except for the fact that it was landlocked, it appeared to be a little bit like heaven. Our plan was to find a farm that needed tender loving care, fix it up and then hold our wedding ceremony on the property. We drove up every week-end looking at real estate and staying in charming little inns. We were falling in love again, and the pain and anger seemed to fade with each passing day. During those months, I felt more grounded and a part of the real world. I was hard at work in my office in Manhattan when the happy call came. Peter was in the Berkshires and called excitedly to say he had found it!

"There is no doubt in my mind, this is it!" he exclaimed. "It has a barn, a guest house, eight acres and a great old main house. It needs a lot of work, but if it didn't we'd never be able to afford it. What do you think?"

In my gut I felt that it was right so I told him to go ahead, even though I knew I wouldn't get a chance to see it for another week. We made a bid, and before I knew it, we were moving. Fortunately, Peter had described it perfectly, and I loved it just as much as he did.

Moving day was a cold, clear March morning. As we pulled away from the city, a heavy weight left my shoulders. I knew we had a lot of hard work ahead of us, but it was fun work because we would be doing it together. The truck with all our belongings arrived on schedule and we began to unload as snowflakes began to fall. How charming, we thought. Could anything be more picturesque? The gentle snowfall soon turned into a major storm that locked us in for three days. We had no food and very little wood for the stove. The closest market was twenty-seven miles away. We were having our first country adventure, and in this part of the country, Domino's doesn't deliver.

A few weeks after closing on the house, I was laid-off from my job in the City. It actually came as a welcomed relief. I was not looking forward to commuting, and I knew I would qualify for unemployment benefits until I could find something in the area. Peter and I eagerly tackled the massive renovation. We cut aged barn wood for the kitchen cabinets, stripped and sanded all the hardwood floors, and even built a brick hearth for the wood stove. All the pieces were falling into place. Our "handyman special" house was quickly becoming a beautiful home. On the recommendation from a city friend, I landed a job at an Equity theater company as their Marketing and Development Director, and Peter started house painting with a local contractor. The house was shaping up. We now had some money coming in, and our wedding day was quickly approaching. So why did I feel such a sense of doom? I kept myself so busy that there was little time to think. I didn't want to hear what my inner voice was saying or what the pain in my body might mean. I wanted a simple life in the country and that was what I was going to have. As usual, my willfulness pushed resolutely ahead, but destiny would not let it stray too far before it brought me to a screeching halt.

The marriage was a disaster from the start. We fought just minutes after the ceremony. Instead of experiencing joy in our union, it reignited a power-struggle between our egos. Even the reception was a disappointment. The barbecued chicken was inedible, a poignant metaphor for how Peter and I felt, burnt on the outside and raw on the inside. Our honeymoon took place on Montauk, Long Island. Friends of my family lent us their beautifully romantic beach house that sat high atop the dunes overlooking the Atlantic Ocean. While piloting the small plane that brought us there, Peter wrenched his back. The honeymoon consisted of frequent visits to the chiropractor and dining every night as a threesome with Pete's buddy from L.A., who was also visiting. Peter's back was so badly in spasm that he could not make it upstairs to the master bedroom. Instead he opted for a single bed in a guest room on the ground floor. I spent hours by myself walking the beach and exploring the surrounding landscape. It was to become an important symbol of the way the marriage was to be: lonely.

The events surrounding our marriage and honeymoon would not have been so devastating but for the fact that neither one of us was happy. Peter's anger was back with a vengeance and I was the target. I realized he had never forgiven me for leaving him and running off with Rene. Sometimes I felt the reason he married me was just to punish me for what I had done. The tragedy was that he was punishing himself as well. Time passed and we tried to make the best of it, but it was taking its toll on us both. My only hope for the marriage was that perhaps by starting a family we could retrieve our love again.

My female problems were becoming frequent and painful and I had no luck conceiving. The more I tried to get pregnant the sicker I became until the pain was so severe that I could no longer have intercourse. My doctor in the Berkshires recommended surgery and possibly a hysterectomy. I called my old doctor in Long Island for a second opinion. Unfortunately, he agreed with the preliminary diagnosis. He felt there might be a possibility of uterine cancer, and that to delay would be foolhardy. I trusted him and decided to have the surgery on Long Island the following month. I knew that if he didn't have to perform a hysterectomy, he wouldn't. He would honor my wishes and it was worth the hassle and the long drive to be assured of that. I knew that cutting everything out of me was not the answer. I just wasn't sure what was.

The surgery yielded little relief. I was diagnosed with severe endometriosis, a condition in which endometrial tissue backs up through the fallopian tubes and into the pelvis, often causing infertility and pain. The condition had also spread to my bladder. I lost part of my left ovary and the right one was becoming encased as well. My doctor said there was little he could do if I was not willing to have a hysterectomy or experiment with male hormones. He said the hormones were sometimes effective in arresting the disease, but the side effects could be considerable. Neither of these options appealed to me. I knew in my heart that this disease was happening for a reason and that the healing would be found when I understood the cause. My womb was crying out for help and I needed to answer that call. I tried everything, from kelp shakes and Chinese herbs to yoga and fasting. I spent two years going to non-traditional doctors, healers, psychics, homeopaths and nutritionists. Nothing worked. I just kept getting sicker and sicker. The pain was becoming more severe and I was bleeding all the time. I became anemic and very weak. I felt that if I didn't get the answer, I would slowly bleed to death.

When I was a little girl, my father taught me a mind-control technique that he had learned in the Navy during World War II. He called it 'mind over matter.' The Seabees and Marines practiced it to overcome pain or torture in case of capture. I was grateful that I had learned this skill, and I practiced it daily for over two years. One night I was lying on the couch. Peter was out, and I was in a great deal of pain. I began to enter a meditative state when suddenly the air in the room began to tingle with a strange kind of effervescence. Time seemed to stand still. I felt an overwhelming wave of warmth and peace pass over me. Then the most wonderful thing occurred. I looked up to see what I can only describe as an angel standing over me. He was very tall and I remember thinking to myself that in all the world I had never seen anything to compare with his beauty.

He leaned towards me and whispered, "Do not be afraid, this pain will pass and you will be all right. You need merely think of me and I will comfort you." He smiled and touched my shoulder with his hand. His gentle touch filled me with an electric feeling of Divine love. Tears of joy began to pour down my face and a sensation of intense ecstasy swirled around and through my whole being. I thought that what I was feeling went beyond human knowledge. It was as though I had somehow been lifted out of my body and onto another plane. What I felt was not earthly, and my mind had trouble fully comprehending it. For those few ecstatic moments, I had been taken to a Heavenly plane and showered with the grace of God. All fear left me, and as quickly as He came He was gone. I didn't know it then, but I would meet this Angel again and learn his true identity at a later time.

Lying there afterwards I looked around the room. Nothing had changed. My dog Tosha was still sleeping and the cold wind outside continued to howl, but my body was pulsating from head to toe. The awareness of my physical pain was still there, but I felt very removed from it. What is this pain, and what is it trying to tell me? Have I been so busy trying to control it that I missed the whole point of why it is here? "Yes!" resonated through me. Then a question came to mind that would take many years to answer, but it was truly the beginning of my healing process. Why was I trying to strangle the life out of my womb? I realized that the endometriosis had covered my entire uterus, and the pain was caused by it squeezing and tightening around my womb and bladder. At that moment, I knew that when I could answer that question, the endometriosis would be gone. I felt elated at this revelation. I knew I would find the answer and that I would be healed.

Weeks passed and outwardly I appeared to become sicker, but I knew that no matter what happened, my angel would be with me. I wished that Peter and I had been closer so that I could share my experience with him. Instead, I sensed that he had begun fantasizing about my death. I knew that when I got better, I would have to leave the marriage. He wanted it to be over, it needed to be over, and no one was at fault. It was just not meant to be. It took me a long time to realize the wrong that I did to Peter by trying to use him to fulfill my fantasy of domestic tranquillity. I had used my will selfishly and that was a deep violation that karmically I would have to amend.

A second surgery found no cancer, but the doctor said that I was most likely sterile and that there was nothing more they could do. The emotional pain of knowing that I would never have children was even worse than the physical pain, and I would have to deal with them both alone. My beautiful dream of having a family was officially over, and so was my marriage.

There was nothing left to do but let go. So I did.

Chapter Six

Alone

The farm sold quickly, and I bought a small cottage on a river bank about ten miles closer to town. The sound of water was healing as it filled the little house I named BabbleBrook. The divorce was conducted in a civilized manner with all our possessions equally divided. Like a flash flood, the marriage began and ended in less than three years. All that remained was the aftermath of pain and a photo album of happier times. All those pictures that once represented everything suddenly were no longer appropriate. It reminded me of when my parents had died. I packed up their clothes and took the boxes off to Goodwill. After all the years of glamour and grandiosity, their lives were reduced to a car load of cartons. I had spent so much time trying to build a foundation for my life, and now another house of cards had fallen.

Once again my self-will led to suffering and heartache. No matter how much I fought, destiny always had its way. Here I was alone again, facing the decision to surrender to God's will. The second challenge was not simply to break ties with Rene and the film, but to surrender my stubborn willfulness and listen to my inner voice.

Humiliated by the failed marriage, I made a commitment to celibacy. Relationships were always my downfall, perhaps because I never established a true relationship with myself. I had been so busy fighting for what I wanted that I never stopped to consider what was best for me. I looked for love outside of myself because it did not exist within. Ioch's words came to mind, "Nothing outside of yourself exists. The outer world is merely a reflection of your inner world. If you seek anything outside of yourself, emptiness will be the result. How could it be otherwise?" With that realization I made a vow that until I could love myself unconditionally, I would not enter into another relationship with anyone. It had been easy to lose myself in the material world, but to go inside and intimately know myself was a frightening prospect. My reluctance seemed odd when I considered the fact that a relationship with myself was the only one that would last. If I didn't know myself, how could I know what was right for me? Perhaps this lack of understanding was the basis of all my unhappiness.

In Egypt as an initiate, I lacked the inner foundation that would have supported me through my Trials. Did Ptah-stepenu and Ioch know of my shortcomings? I was swept away, my shallow roots unable to hold during the storm of temptation that Raji-Amen had orchestrated. Where was my Being, that wise, eternal part of me, when my human self was falling so blindly? Why was I not able to access my inner wisdom or the aid of my teachers? If I were to be free from the effects of this blindspot, it would be crucial to understand and to heal it.

Before Tenu was to take the Secret Tenets to safety, I spoke with him in the garden. He seemed so calm and secure in his beliefs. I was not at peace, neither in his passing nor when the door to the initiation chamber closed behind me. Everything that I loved was outside that cold, lonely tomb except for the child that lay dying in my womb. As I waited for death to come, my heart felt I was being sacrificed for the Son's of God. My love for them made it worth the price, but it seemed a huge cost. Since I did not have a strong enough sense of my true Self, I missed the whole point. The belief in sacrifice only exists in the unhealed personality of the ego. To the pure of heart, sacrifice does not exist. In the beginning, my heart had been pure, but it could not stay that way because I lacked wisdom. Purity must be guarded if it is to be preserved.

Tenu was at peace because he was doing his duty to God, and therefore blessing, not sacrificing, himself. His purity brought him joy. In Egypt, I was not able to fulfill my duty to God and in this life my duty seemed like a burden. Based on a fragmented self, how could it not? I realized that I had to heal my personality before I could transcend it. I thought that I could reach for God and be uplifted over the pain of childhood, my misperceptions, self-doubt, and fear. I could not. The journey lay within, and it was the last place on earth I wanted to visit. The blackness I felt inside far exceeded anything I had experienced in the pit of darkness.

Then I had a startling thought. Maybe we carry the pit of darkness inside of us until we are willing to do battle with it. Is that what denial is really about, avoiding the challenges within? Are compulsive behavior, codependence, and self-hate rooted in this elaborate deception? This insight resonated as truth in my heart. I began to understand that the pit of darkness was not in my tomb in Egypt or deep within the bowels of Cairo airport. It was in me. Each of us carries it with us until we find the courage to fight the noble battle of light. The longer we delay, the deeper we sink into addiction, isolation, self-destruction and war. That was what Ioch was trying to tell me when he said, "Trust the truth and not the illusion. If you fall for the illusion, it will overtake you."

In desperation I prayed: "Ioch, my blessed teacher, have I been mistaken all these years? Is the journey in fact a journey within ourselves, to the core of darkness that we hold inside our minds?" I waited for his reply and after so many years of silence, he was there. My heart leapt with relief and gratitude.

"You have discovered the root of all human fear, the false belief that you are separate from God (and alone in the darkness forever). You began your journey within when the memory of Egypt surfaced. From the moment of remembering in the Great Pyramid until seven years have passed you will remain in the lessons of the pit of darkness. If you have been successful at the end of the seven years, a great Light will enter your being and you will be lifted up. To free yourself completely from the power of the darkness, you must complete all of the Trials. Success does not mean perfection. That is not possible. It does mean, however, an understanding of the lessons, a demonstration of practicing these lessons, and overcoming these challenges in your daily actions and inner thoughts. The crystal Black Obsidian holds within its properties the clues. The Seven Trials must be faced and overcome in order to free yourself from the power of the dark forces. Once you have accomplished this, you will no longer be challenged by the darkness because you will have developed the skill to see beyond it to the light."

"Ioch," I said, "I would like to name these Trials the Obsidian Trials, for they are like gazing into the blackness of the stone and suddenly seeing more light than darkness and then, eventually, seeing only the light."

Ioch agreed and then continued: "As a young girl your perception was still primarily on the linear plane, or more specifically, an attachment to the three-dimensional world of the senses. You were able to see the fourth dimension, but still not able to be at one with it. Since your birth you have been able to hear our voices, and occasionally see one of us, but there was a veil between our worlds.

"As you have grown and overcome the lures of addiction and worldly despair, the veil was slowly lifted. We are now reunited and here to help you. As a being in physical form you need the clarity and aid of the fourth dimension. This is in order to fully overcome the Obsidian Trials for they encompass your greatest fears. Before you came to earth for this lifetime, you made a commitment to us and, bless you, you have kept your promise.

"The Obsidian Trials will be overcome, or they will overcome you as they did long ago in Egypt. The battle of darkness and light is really the only battle there is. In your childhood you were surrounded by darkness. The light within seemed dim and powerless, but your faith prevailed and the light in your heart expanded until your twenty-eighth year, when you were able to overcome the darkness and let the grace of God bless you. It all began when you surrendered your addiction of alcohol to God. The admission of power-lessness and your willingness to let go is what saved you."

I protested: "But I did not really surrender. I had been drinking the same as always and a Voice came to me and told me that it was all over. I haven't had a drink since. It was lifted from me."

"This is very true, Santi, but you forget the important role your mother's death played in your healing. Do you remember how afraid she was and how your presence helped to ease those fears so that she could die at peace?"

"Yes, but what does that have to do with my drinking?"

Ioch continued: "In the last few moments of her life as you held her hand and spoke to her of God, you saw her drawn and painful face suddenly glow with a brilliant light that allowed her beauty to emerge once more. It was so beautiful that you wanted that light within you and prayed to God for it. Your mother may have given you a lot of pain in this lifetime, but in that moment she gave you a tremendous gift. She showed you the truth about life, and about love. Your prayer was your surrender, and you prayed for the light for many years before your release. Addiction of any kind begets darkness. When you wanted the light that showed in your mother's dying face, the healing process was allowed to begin within you.

Victory over attachment was complete the day you stopped drinking. You then moved up to the next level, facing Trial Number One immediately. Addictive and compulsive behavior is a major symptom of a person lost in desire and need. Remember that the sole purpose of this lesson is to bring the wants and needs, or desires, of the ego under the guidance and control of the spirit. To the extent that the individual gives his or her power to the ego, the deeper he or she will be immersed in addictive, compulsive behavior with an external dependency and a self-centered perception. This downward spiral leads us further from our spiritual nature until only a vivid awareness of the destructive nature of our will and a complete willingness to surrender will free us. When the individual no longer chooses to employ the ego as his or her master and instead turns to God for direction, he or she has completed this lesson, which is often experienced as a rebirth. As the veil begins to lift, this can be accompanied by powerful spiritual experiences. After each victory there follows a period of grace and rest, but this does not last long, for the challenges of the next lesson now face the initiate."

Still needing clarity, I asked Ioch to explain the Seven Obsidian Trials in detail. "You said that it would take me seven years from the time that I was in Egypt to complete these Trials. Several years have passed. I need to know where I am in the process."

Ioch answered immediately. "Santi, you are further along than you realize. Your expectations are so high that you often miss the sweetness of the moment."

"Trial Number One: *Surrendering all forms of desire to God*. Your desire for self will and control was surrendered when you turned your alcoholism and your will over to God. Your desire for Rene - the financial security and the power - were challenges that you successfully completed by walking away from all of them. You proved that you desire God more than the offerings of the ego.

"Trial Number Two: *The fear of losing all your worldly possessions*. You overcame this by breaking the contract with Rene, knowing that it would totally drain your

resources. You appeared to lose everything, but you accurately realized the loss was only of possessions and the illusion of security. This was a great victory that helped establish non-attachment in your being. In order to be free, you gave up everything and held nothing back, thereby freeing yourself from the Second Trial.

"Trial Number Three: <u>*Non-attachment to the transitory aspects of the world*</u>. The challenge here was to accept that you were not meant to have children in this lifetime. You were trying to bargain with God, foolishly believing that pleading and justifying had some affect. The result was that you sank deeper into illusion and despair. If it is not aligned with God's will, self-will always produces pain and suffering. Pain and suffering are not inflicted by God; they are always self-inflicted. It is only when one works and lives in cooperation with the Creator that pain and suffering fall away. Take responsibility for what you have created. Evaluate its results based on whether or not it produces peace. You will then be free to co-create with God. Your fear is merely the result of believing in your ego rather than in God. When we attach ourselves and our happiness to things that do not last, we are put in a state of perpetual fear. The ego tries to squelch the fear by exerting its control over the situation. This may appear to be a solution, but only temporarily. Ultimately, it never lasts. The fear always returns when the object that we are attached to is gone. You perceived the death of your parents and other family members as a great loss, but you have not lost them nor they you. You can never lose their spirit. The form will change and fall away, but the spirit - never. You have learned to let go of the changeable aspect of things while giving your heart to its essence. That is the light in the Third Trial and that is why you are free from it.

"*Trial Number Four*: <u>*To be of one mind with God, free from the personal will of the ego*</u>. You cannot serve two Masters any more than you can walk in two different directions at the same time. God is not demanding that we serve Him. If you would rather serve yourself, by all means do so. That is what free will is all about. If you choose the ego, know fully what you are choosing, for the ego comes with its companions; fear, doubt and lovelessness. No lasting peace crosses the brow of a person who is ruled by his or her intellect alone. God's path is not an easy one. As we learned in the first three lessons, uprooting the ego and the attachments to the world is a painful and unsettling process. Loneliness is the first symptom of Trial Four, but the deepest pain will be met by an even greater love and comfort, if the individual is willing to give his or her life over completely to the Creator. God is your Father. He created you for Glory, not despair. Would any of us turn away from God if we knew what he wanted for us?

"You must face the essence of every fear your mind holds to be true, for if your mind holds it to be true then that is where you have placed your trust and that must be corrected. These circumstances you perceive as painful will soon be transformed into precious pieces of peace and joy. The Obsidian Trials are absolute. First you must face that which you fear. Then you must come to understand the truth about that fear before it can be released. The truth about any event that occurs is that it has within it the seeds for transformation. To give your life to God, therefore, is to be transformed and free from the laws that govern the ego and the world.

"Trial Number Five: <u>*Surrendering all pain to God without reservation*</u>. The angel came to you after many years of agonizing pain with endometriosis because in your heart you were able to look past the disease and its effects to the question of its true purpose. You detached from your body and began to identify yourself more as a spiritual being in an evolutionary experience rather than a physical being weakened by disease. Your ability to access your true nature summoned the angel to come and comfort you. He has been with

you all this time, but could not assist you without permission. Permission was granted when you opened the door to your true Self."

Ioch paused and in his sweetest voice aid, "Pray to see the truth and not the illusion, no matter how powerful the deception appears. Study the laws of the Obsidian Stone. It will help you understand that no matter how dark the path, you will not walk it alone. There are powerful guardians to assist you. Be still and you will hear them. Be open and you will know them."

Silence fell like the curtain at the end of a play that you wish would go on forever. He was gone. Ioch said that the seven challenges of the pit of darkness would last seven years, and then there would be a great light to lift me up to the next Trial. I would have two more Trials before me. I knew in my heart that the deepest, darkest fears still lay ahead, and I had only the most minute understanding of the first five Trials. How could I do this? Help me, my angels. Just as the fear was about to take hold, I remembered when I lay dying in the tomb in Egypt, a woman's voice so strong and familiar comforted me and proclaimed the truth of my being. "You are a fortress, a warrior, and the unattached defender of the Law of One." Was she one of the guardians here to help me? I prayed to her to help find the warrior within me, for I knew the battlefield was on the horizon. The Obsidian Trials were surrounding me, and my opponent, fear, was everywhere.

The next day I went to the crystal store to find a book about the crystal obsidian. Shelves were cluttered with every new age book imaginable, most of which I had already read. Even my house was filled with books on God and philosophy. As a little girl I would lie on the grass on cool summer evenings and stare up at the stars, wondering where I had come from and why I was here. Hours would pass, and then years, but the answers still eluded me. When I got to the section that I was looking for, a book immediately leapt out at me: Katrina Raphaell's, <u>Crystal Enlightenment, The Transforming Properties of Crystals and Healing Stones</u>. I turned to the index, and sure enough, there was a section on the black obsidian. I hurriedly flipped through the pages marked "new age stones," and there it was. I began to read:

> Black Obsidian's purpose is to take the mind through the darkened areas of the subconscious to establish identity in the super-conscious... It acts as a mirror that reflects the flaws in one's nature and magnifies the fears, insecurities and egocentric attitudes that suppress the soul's superior qualities. Black Obsidian could be named the "warrior of truth," that which slays the illusion to give birth to the vision of the Aquarian Age.

The essence of the learning just as Ioch had said: to find the light in the darkness. I bought the book and a small piece of this mysterious stone to add to my ever-expanding crystal collection. I loved crystals and displayed them all over my house. This stone, however, felt different, as if it asked me to go back to my childhood, a place to which I swore never to return. My head began to reel. With so much information to assimilate, I felt weary and went home to rest. Almost instantly I fell into a deep sleep, dreaming a recurrent dream I had experienced many times throughout childhood.

It was a beautiful summer day. My mother and I were walking along the high cliffs above the sea picking wildflowers. She walked ahead while I was lost in song and happiness. The sun was warm, and its bright light made the sea sparkle. The clean sea air seemed to purify my body. I walked hurriedly up the hill, but my little legs could not keep up with my mother's long, strong stride. At the top of the hill, much to my surprise, were four Grecian white marble statues of men, their nude, muscular bodies strangely cold and uninviting. I continued to pick flowers, my mother still walking far ahead. I never saw her face, but she was dressed in white, her black hair cascading down her back. I called for her to wait, but she did not appear to hear me. A chill went up my back. It felt as though I was being stared at. I turned to see if someone was there.

Suddenly, the statues came to life, and began to chase me with devouring eyes. I screamed to my mother for help, but she simply gazed out to sea. I tried to run as fast as I could towards her, but my feet felt like lead. Terrified and exhausted, I finally reached her, grabbing her arms for protection and safety. These madmen were just a few paces behind, "Mother help me! What's wrong with you?" I screamed. Slowly, she turned, looking at me with cold, hateful eyes just like those of the men. With great delight she laughed - a sinister, bloodcurdling laugh that struck at the heart of my soul. The men enthusiastically joined her. I was surrounded by them, my feet teetering at the edge of the cliffs. There was nowhere to go, and no escape. Why did such an insane situation feel so familiar? Their sharp, jagged fingernails sunk into my flesh. With great force, they began to push me over the cliff. I could not hold on. I felt myself falling faster and faster until my body smashed onto the sharp, jagged rocks below, taking my breath away. I knew I was dying. With a last upward glance, I saw them all laughing high up on the cliffs. The dream went black and the pounding of my heart woke me.

I sat up in bed covered in cold sweat and trembling from head to toe. That damned nightmare again. I hadn't had it in years. Part of me wanted to know what it meant, but another part felt terrified of discovering what this dream was trying to tell me. I thought that I had worked through all of that childhood stuff. During the past five years, I attended workshops for Adult Children of Alcoholics, twelve step groups, support groups, and private therapy. How much more could I do? It seemed obvious by my reaction to the dream and my resistance to going within, that there was something that needed to be looked at. I was still in severe pain from the endometriosis, and the question continued to haunt me.

My psychotherapist suggested that I go on a solitary retreat. It was something she did on a regular basis and recommended highly. At first it did not sound like something I needed to do, since I already spent most of my time alone. Why travel fifty miles to a retreat center, to sit and be alone? She assured me, however, that there was a world of difference between being alone and conscious stillness. Everything else I had tried hadn't worked, so I decided to give it a try. I became gratefully aware that my desire to heal was greater than my fear of what I might discover buried in my past. I called the retreat center, and made a reservation for that weekend. Three days would be about all that I could handle for my first retreat.

The day quickly arrived, and I packed everything I thought I might need for the wilderness. Fall weather was unpredictable and I hated being cold. In addition to clothing, I had to pack enough dry food. There would be no electricity, no refrigeration, and only a wood stove for heat. I'm glad I didn't know beforehand that there was also no bathroom and no water except for the bucket at the well about a quarter of a mile away.

After traveling down numerous dirt roads, I saw a sign instructing me to park the car and continue the rest of the way on foot. I had no idea how I would carry everything I had packed. I combed through my backpack and duffel bag, unloading extra sweaters and slacks. Eventually, I pared it down and began the mile walk that led up a very steep trail. Stopping from time to time to catch my breath, I thought of the burdens that we carry with us through life. Did I really need all these things? Was my love of comfort and fear of hunger so strong that I had to carry twice what I actually needed, just in case?

It seemed to take all afternoon, but I finally arrived at a huge gong. A sign said to ring the gong and wait for someone to escort you to your cabin. My pack felt as if there were bricks in it so I was actually glad to have an opportunity to sit on the ground and wait. Soon a woman greeted me. She was about my age, but she appeared to have been frozen in the sixties. I was given a list of the rules which included total silence and respect for all living things. I had no problem with that, having secretly yearned for real peace and quiet. Even as a child I had been sensitive to noise. This would probably be the first time I would experience complete silence for three solid days.

The paths were clearly marked with blue paint on tree bark. The outhouse was clean and screened, with a St. Francis prayer beside a wax candle. I began to relax, and slow down. My cabin was beautiful. It had large windows, a wood stove, a small altar area, and a futon for sitting and sleeping. I was home. "I can heal here," I thought. "This will be my healing sanctuary."

The first night was uneventful. I was so exhausted from traveling and hiking that sleep was foremost in my mind. I awoke next day to a crimson sunrise in the mountain mist. I started a fire in the stove, and then trotted over to the out house. It was my first morning in the woods. I felt grateful that I had been led to this place. After some yoga stretches and a light breakfast, I took a long hike to a look-out spot where I decided to sit and meditate. The sun was still in the East, and I could feel it on my back. In no time at all, I sank into a deep state of relaxation.

A flyer for a yoga therapy training kept coming to mind. I had first seen it displayed at the printers when I was having some brochures made for work. I felt compelled to take it and asked the person behind the counter if I could have a copy. Yoga has always been a part of my life. My mother was my first teacher, although she joked that she would find me doing yoga in my crib. The thought of becoming a certi-fied instructor interested me. The real pull came, however, from the man who was directing the program, Michael Lee or

Ramanath, his sanskrit name. He looked so familiar. I felt the moment I saw his picture that someday we would work together. It made little sense, but I had no doubts. His face and the name of his school, Phoenix Rising, kept flowing in and out of consciousness for the remainder of the meditation. I resolved that when I returned to the Berkshires, I would call and arrange a meeting with him.

The weekend was profoundly restful and clarifying. I knew that I wanted to begin the necessary steps to leave the theater and go into the healing profession. I wanted to be of service in any way that I could. I would begin with this yoga training and see where it led.

I called Michael Lee bright and early Monday morning and told him about my experience at the printers. He was pleasant and open to meeting with me. Phoenix Rising was located only a few blocks from the theater in Stockbridge so I went over on my lunch hour. I liked him instantly, and again my inner voice kept insisting that we were going to work together one day. I felt so comfortable with Michael that I finally told him what my guidance was saying. He did not seem surprised by my remarks, and in his charming Australian accent said, "If it is meant to be, it will be." I signed up for his class and the next certification course.

Soon I was teaching Michael's yoga class whenever he was out of town, a class he eventually turned over to me. The yoga therapy training was all I hoped it would be, and more. The work was intense and profound. It was during the training that I became aware of how little I had literally been present in my body. Mentally and spiritually I traveled to great depths, but physically I stayed pretty much on the surface. I was very protective of my body and never participated in any sport that would put it at risk. My tolerance for physical pain had been lowered after years of physical abuse by my mother in her drunken rages. When she hit me I would retreat into my mind for escape. Although she tried to hurt me with cruel insults and humiliating remarks, I felt safe. Now I was taking a course that specifically focused on the body, and how we hold trauma in the cells of our own body. Old emotions were being stirred up and something was getting ready to be released. I felt vulnerable and tears of an unexplained origin were easily triggered throughout the day. My image of being strong and having it all together was coming apart at the seams. My ego wanted to run away, but my heart knew I was on the right track for healing.

My good friend Emily was also taking the certification training, and we traded yoga therapy sessions. We had both completed levels one and two. Level Three, the final level, required a certain number of sessions to be given and then received so that we could experience what our clients would be experiencing. This was a very intense part of the process, because the techniques bring up buried trauma if the client is willing to let go of the holding in the body and embrace the process. I knew in my heart that I could only take a client as far as I had gone in my own healing, so this was a great incentive for me to delve into my own psyche. It was my turn to receive a session. I was looking forward to the sense of relaxation that follows a good release. I was doing an average of two hours of yoga a day, so I was in great shape and felt very limber. This made the sessions even more beneficial because when relaxed, the body can more easily let go into the posture. The muscles fight the process when they are stiff.

Emily thought she would try some new techniques, and just play around with various postures to see what would happen. That sounded fine with me so I started by lying on my back. She was just going to stretch my arms and legs out as far as they would go to open up the trunk of the body. She began with my legs. She lifted the right leg straight up in the air and then, supporting the knee, guided the leg towards my head for a nice hamstring stretch. Then she took the leg from side to side opening any holding in the hips as the extended leg lengthened along the floor. My mind was letting go and my whole lower body was releasing and opening.

I sank like a stone into relaxation and peace. She finished stretching both legs and then took both my arms into her hands with a firm grip. She pulled them up in front of me, and then began to lengthen them by pulling them over my head behind me. I became agitated which seemed odd after having been so relaxed. As she continued to intensify the pull, fear welled up and a sense of panic filled my whole being. I felt as if I had entered an altered state of consciousness. My breathing changed and Emily noticed my shift, but she continued to stretch my arms. My arm pit filled with heat and a sense of tissue ripping. The odd thing about this sensation was that it did not feel like it was happening in the present. I was experiencing a cellular trauma from the past. I had heard Michael talk about it, but had not had the experience until now. It felt eerie, and staying present was a real challenge.

Just as I was getting used to this odd occurrence, something I could not stay with began to happen. I started to see knives coming at me. It didn't matter whether I had my eyes opened or closed. There they were. I began gasping for air. Emily released my arms and I began to cry. She left me alone, realizing that I could not tell her what was going on even if I had wanted to. I had to recuperate first and get grounded again. The images of the knives finally subsided and I quieted down. I described to her as best I could what had happened, but even I was not sure what it meant. I only knew that when she stretched and extended my left arm, something was triggered in the tissue on the underside.

I left the session completely drained, feeling a need to be alone. I thought if I rested I could leave this experience behind me. Much to my horror, that was not to be the case. Every time I made the transition from wakefulness to sleep, the knife images would come into view. I tried praying for help, but nothing changed. In fact, they became more vivid and terrifying. Was I losing my mind?

Back in the Berkshires, I spoke to my therapist about it and she offered her usual suggestion. "If there is something your subconscious wants to tell you, it will come up if you sit long enough. You keep running from it and it keeps following you. Why don't you stop running?" Her words were scary to hear, but they rang true. I remembered in Elisabeth Haich's book, "Initiation", that she went on an extended retreat to learn of the path that she was to take in life. It had a profound effect on her life and the choices she made. I had been going on retreat regularly since that first time, and instead of resisting, I welcomed the peace and serenity they offered. Once a month I would go for a three-day weekend. I had a regular cabin which was named Pine, appropriately nestled amongst them in a giant pine forest. I called to reserve the space, but this time I wanted it for an undesignated amount of time. I made a commitment to stay as long as I needed, in order to have this memory surface. My resolution outweighed my fear, but not by much.

Chapter Seven

Unbound

The day dawned cold and foreboding as an early winter storm made it's way into our corner of the world. It seemed as though this part of New England had only two seasons instead of the usual four, namely winter and summer. As I made my way up the mountain the last quarter mile felt endless. My backpack felt like a boulder that strained my back and breath. The thought of the wood stove blazing and a cup of hot tea helped to cope with plummeting temperatures and very thin air. The image of a cup of tea has often helped me through difficult situations. My English blood has served well in times of stress. I detoured off the main trail to take a shortcut to pine grove. From there it was just a few hundred yards through the woods. Ice formed on the ground, making it hard to climb. A burst of stubborn energy helped me make it to the crest where I could see Pine's chimney in the distance.

The challenge of the climb had temporarily distracted me from the reason I was here, but as I neared my cabin, a feeling of dread surrounded me. Another Obsidian Trial was about to begin. I could feel it. The darkness fueled my fear, but now I had experience as an ally. The darkness would come and appear to be all that existed. If I focused on the blackness it would expand like oil in water. The challenge was to look for the light in the black, and then watch the light expand as darkness suddenly would be expelled. The knives and what they were trying to tell me seemed frightening in their form, so darkness surrounded their message. I would face them head-on, praying to see the truth and the light.

At last I arrived at the cabin. I dropped my pack on the floor and quickly built a fire in the stove. Except for the biting wind, it felt almost as cold inside as out. My body began to relax as the wood crackled and smoke rose up the chimney. Once the fire was set, I would go to the well for water. Even though the well was a good distance from the cabin, the terrain was flat and somewhat sheltered from the wind Again the thought of hot tea and honey spurred me on. As I sat comfortably in front of the blazing stove sipping my tea, I was filled with gratitude. The retreats in this cabin were healing in so many ways. I could slow down enough to really enjoy such simplicity. The tea, the stove's heat, the oil lamp, all unsurpassed pleasures to comfort and soothe as the wind echoed the coyotes' cry.

I was safe here, and I knew my beloved Ioch was watching over me. How blessed I am. My pain has always been matched with equal gifts of joy. In the past, I was too afraid to trust any gifts except fear and pain. Bliss was tough medicine to swallow. Happily, that distortion was beginning to heal and I could more easily let God's love into my heart. I could feel God in the warmth of the fire, in the pleasure of the rice and beans and in the promise of a deep and restful sleep after a long day. But could I feel him in the terror of the knives? Hardly. Yet I knew that God must be everywhere, or He is nowhere. I had no doubt that God existed. Since my earliest recollection, there has not been a moment when I have not felt His presence in my life. If I could allow myself to feel God while I remembered the knives, I could get through this. The challenge was to focus on God, not on the knives. Ioch's words came to mind: "The light always dispels the darkness." My commitment was so strong that courage and self-respect began to flood my being. I felt my honor return. As I rolled out my sleeping bag and turned down the lamp, I felt like one of King Arthur's knights resting before his search for the Holy Grail continued. The moon was coming up and snowflakes were gathering on the skylight as I drifted off to sleep.

Three days passed, and I continued to pray and meditate as the image of knives filled my mind. I felt weary and hopeless. Would I ever be able to remember what happened? Maybe I was just crazy, and there was nothing to remember. I could not accept that my guidance had led me to a dead end, and yet I felt stuck in a draining, fearful limbo. Evening was approaching, and I had to gather firewood. I bundled up and headed to pine grove for some kindling. The moon was low in the sky, appearing twice its normal size. I have always loved basking in the moonlight, feeling the blue light through the tree shadows. I suddenly dropped down on my knees and began to pray,

> *Holy Spirit of God, how deeply I love you, and how grateful I am for Your Grace. Hold me in Your loving arms and guide me through to the other side. I am tired of being afraid. I am tired of being less than I am. I am tired of carrying someone else's shame. I declare before all of my angels, I will not allow the darkness in myself, or in someone else to keep me from my Father's loving destiny. I was not born to be loyal to another's illness. I am loyal to my Father God, and to the spirit of Him that lives and breathes within me. I break allegiance with everything else. Ioch, I know that you are listening. I hold this twig in my hand as a symbol of the Sant, the sacred scepter. I am now ready to serve.*

Holding the twig high in the air towards the moon I felt a current of electricity move down throughout my body. I was ready to remember. I gathered up my kindling and went back to the cabin.

I sat for hours as the moon passed through the sky. Just as my weary back was about to give out, I felt the approaching tremor of impending terror. Like the rising sound of an approaching train, it was coming. Faster...closer...louder. And suddenly, it burst upon me like a tempest and the memories came rushing in.

I was six years old and at home with my mother. I am not sure if I was off from school that day or too young to attend. My sister, who was three years older, had left to catch the bus. Dad was at work. I heard my mother downstairs in the kitchen, screaming and banging things about. I cautiously made my way down the stairs. I wanted to peek in and see what is going on without her noticing me. I looked in to see her drinking her bottle of rye. After a couple of swigs, she poured some into her coffee cup and put the bottle away. Murmuring under her breath, she threw things into the sink, breaking some glass in the process. She staggered over to the table and spotted me. I started heading up the stairs, but she managed to grab the hem of my nightgown, ripping the lace trim. "What are you doing, spying on me?" she snarled. "You come down here my little curse. Nothing has gone well since you were born. We were so happy until you came along. Then everything turned bad. I was always beautiful and healthy. No matter how pretty you think you are, you will never be as pretty or smart as me. Your father doesn't care about me anymore. He is running around, you know."

I didn't understand what she was talking about. She had a crazed look in her eye, as if she was possessed. My real mother, the sober one, was gone and I didn't know how to get her back. This mother reminded me of the wicked witch in the Wizard of Oz. She screamed louder and louder, blaming me for a hysterectomy she'd recently had. Over and over again, she kept saying the surgery was my fault, that she should do the same to me, just to even the score. I didn't know what she meant, but I was terrified of the way she looked at me. Her eyes were filled with murderous hate. Did she mean to kill me?

She held a firm grip on my arm, and it felt like it was breaking. She rustled through the drawer. What was she looking for? Then, in a flash, she turned and threw me on the cold porcelain kitchen table. She gathered my arms and hands together and held me firmly. I felt cold and exposed with no means of covering up or getting away. I was horrified and helpless. I felt that my mother was going to kill me. Holding me down with one hand, she reached over to the kitchen drawer once again, and I could see through the reflection in the stainless steel coffeepot that she was reaching for the knife. My heart sank and began to beat so fast I thought it would explode. She turned towards me with a large knife in her hand, screaming about sterilizing me as I had done to her.

I didn't know what any of the words meant. I only knew that feeling of powerless was enough to drive me out of my mind. I swore that if I got out of this alive, I would never allow myself to be helpless again. In my horror, I blacked out. When I came to she was sobbing. I was repulsed by her and only wanted my freedom. If only I could cover up and get away. Please God, help me! She released her grip, kissing me and pleading for my forgiveness. Her old self had returned and she was filled with horror and remorse. I wanted to run and get as far away as I could. She had violated the deepest part of me and tried to destroy me. At that moment, my mother felt dead to me. I would never trust her or anyone else again.

I felt a slight pain in my left side - nothing severe. I realized I had not been hurt physically, but something profound had happened emotionally. From that day forward, I built a wall around myself. I felt hard and detached, no longer a sweet, little girl with sparkling eyes. My mother had betrayed the deepest part of my being and that event marked the beginning of our battle of wills that lasted until a few months before her death when we were able to make peace and forgive one another.

That was the memory that I had blocked all those years. Twenty-five years later, I was sterile, not as a physical result of that incident, but, I believe, as an emotional effect. Her words resonated within, "You deserve to be sterile. It is all your fault that this happened. You need to be punished." Even though I didn't understand her words at the time, on some level they took hold and eventually, I believed them. The power of what we are told as children is profound. My mother's alcoholism destroyed her as well as our relationship. This memory brought with it much understanding about the way I felt and acted in certain situations. My fear of being held down, the way I panic when I am cold or uncovered. With the heartbreak of this memory came a deep validation that I was not crazy. I had simply been deeply wounded with no outer or inner support.

Two years after this event, I was hospitalized with a severe case of nephritis, a serious disease of the kidneys. I was so sick the doctor thought I might die. I remember being very happy at the thought, and wanted to go to Heaven and be with my Father. I knew I would be safe there. Looking back on that time, I never understood why I had wanted to die, and why my kidneys were failing. The Chinese say the kidneys hold our fear. I was certainly holding a toxic amount. I now understood why I had gotten sick. I understood it all. The pain of remembering was soothed by the depth of awareness that came with it. Exhausted, I fell into a deep, restful sleep that would hold me for almost fifteen hours. As I drifted off, Ioch's smiling face filled my mind. I had completed another one of my Trials. I could finally rest in peace. "Thank you, God."

The morning sun was nearly blinding as it reflected through the newly fallen snow. I awoke refreshed, as if a great weight had been lifted. The memory of my mother's violation validated so many feelings and reactions. Most of my life I felt that I might be crazy because of the way that I reacted in certain situations. With this memory, though, I realized my reactions were perfectly understandable. They only appeared crazy because I had blocked the memory. In the morning light the fearful darkness seemed almost silly. What had I been so afraid of?

My stomach was growling, and my bare feet on the cold floor reminded me to stoke up the fire in the wood stove. Mornings on the mountain always felt like the Earth and everything in it was brand new. This morning especially felt like a new beginning, as a painful part of my past could finally be over. I wasn't so naive as to believe that I could just tie this memory up in a neat little ribbon and be done with it. I had a full range of emotions, from relief to killer rage, but I was committed to working through them. At least now I knew what I was working through, and that someday there would be an end to it. All those years in therapy, engulfed in depression, mistrust and despair, I had nothing tangible to attach the feelings to. Now I knew that a lot of what was wrong in my childhood was more complicated than simply being raised in an alcoholic home. My mother's violent rages which escalated along with her drinking binges shattered my sense of safety and trust. It is no wonder that even in early childhood I identified with a line from Dante's "Divine Comedy": "I did not die, but nothing in life remained."

At the age of six, I felt life was over, or perhaps more accurately, I wished that it had been.

What a miracle to feel brand new and ready to claim life! Ioch said that I must first face the fear, and then come to understand the truth about it. It is only then that the fear will be released. Did I see the whole truth about this fear? Is the Trial fearlessly facing a horrifying memory?

Ioch answered immediately: "No, Santi, facing a terrifying event involves surrendering your defenses so that the truth may emerge. The truth is not the memory or the event. The truth is in the energy that needs to be transmitted as a healing light to overcome the dark energy of the violation. Do you understand?"

I heard his words, but their meaning escaped me. I feebly tried to interpret. "The facts of what happened to me are not the lesson. Remembering the facts simply demonstrated my commitment to lowering my defenses so that what was fearfully hidden in my subconscious could surface." In my mind's eye, I see Ioch, nodding. He is pleased with me.

"The details of a person's life are secondary. What truly matters is how they relate to them," I said.

Ioch hesitated: "This is partially true, but you are only scratching the surface. It is an admirable attempt, but the material for the Fifth Trial lies deep within your heart. You will never find it in your mind. Clearing away your armor and willingly making yourself as defenseless as you were when your mother attacked you, will be the challenge in this Trial. You are very strong and smart, my dear Santi. These qualities will work against you in this lesson.

"Although you have achieved the first part of this Fifth Trial, the latter will take a considerable amount of time. The essence of this Trial is something you will never be able to figure out intellectually, although you will most certainly attempt to do just that. This egotism will hinder your progress. The answer will awaken within you, and when it does you will laugh at its simplicity."

That old familiar chill of fear returned, as if the temperature had suddenly dropped thirty degrees. Ioch's voice momentarily diverted me from this bone-chilling cold.

"Santi, what is fearlessness? You will find the answer in your soul's worth, for it is not blind courage or false hope.

When you find it, it will never leave you regardless of the circumstances that lie before you."

I waited for him to say more, but he was gone. Ioch's words left me unsettled. I wanted to shut out our meeting and go back to being excited about the newness and brightness of the day. Fear was such a large part of me. How would I ever be free of it? But that wasn't all that was disturbing. There were a number of feelings, the predominant being disappoint-dment. I had put such importance on remembering what happened in childhood that when the memory surfaced, I felt elated and victorious. I was pleased with my progress, because I thought I was home free, but that simply pulled me back into my ego.

One of my character flaws was often being incorrect about where I stood on the path, seeing myself far ahead or lagging behind. The here and now was often not where I was. The now, which is the only time there is, did not exist because the past and future loomed so large in my perception. I knew Ioch would say that is because I lack faith, that I was still trying to run my life. I have seen progress in myself, but it seems like a snail's pace. I could feel happy about this victory along with being unsettled about my slow spiritual progress. That much I had learned. However, I felt there was a bigger piece to my uneasiness.

When Ioch said that in order to learn this lesson I needed to become as defenseless as I was when my mother hurt me, I felt completely hopeless. In my wildest dreams, I couldn't imagine willingly placing myself in that position again. The thought made me angry and fearful. Instead of lessening my fears, I was creating more of them. How would I ever complete these tasks? It was as though I had been ordered to climb a steep mountain, with bound hands and feet. Ioch's words rang through me: "Even if you are bound you can pray." So I knelt down, and asked for help:

*"Dear Heavenly Father God, I am your servant,
crippled by a relentless ego, but trying to free
myself. Help me. You are my only hope. Help me
to trust that You will not abandon me in my hour of
need. I feel so alone sometimes, like I am lost in
the vastness of space, an endless void where there
is no light, no comfort, and no hope. Help me to
feel my angels' love around me, to hear their
helpful guidance, and to feel the ecstasy of a brush
of their wings. It has been so extreme for me,
Father. Help me find a balance. Most of all,
remind me to look Homeward, for when I do, I am
given the peace I need to go on."*

It was now time to end my retreat, and reenter the world.
I let the fire die out in the wood stove, and headed back to the
Berkshires.

Chapter Eight

The Surrender

My days were becoming fuller. I was in the third phase of my yoga therapy certification, and was seeing clients on a regular basis. Bob Cote, an old friend and clinical director of a substance abuse unit at the local hospital, asked for an appointment for a session. We had taken a lot of workshops together in the past. Bob facilitated a recovery group and felt that some of the body-mind work from yoga therapy training might be interesting and helpful to them. I agreed to do a session with him to see what he thought of the techniques first hand. If he was sufficiently impressed, I would do a body reading demonstration for his group.

Bob came to his appointment not knowing what to expect. I began with some hands on reading just to get a sense of what was happening within his body. Whenever I touched someone, I became aware of aspects about their health and emotions. I had always had psychic ability, even as a child. I never realized that this was a unique gift until my school years. My mother was also gifted in this way. When I was very little we would talk for hours about what we "knew". She was the only person I could discuss this with. Even my father and sister weren't in on our secret talks. Her violation of me was even more devastating because we had been so close. Her drinking destroyed everything - her gifts, our relationship, and eventually her life. I always feared that I might come to the same end. I tried not to be like her, but we were definitely cut from the same mold.

I placed my hands on Bob's back and instantly felt the contraction around his heart. The muscles were tight, as if they had been that way most of his life. I knew that they needed to be released if he was to remain healthy. I asked him to lean back on the pillows behind him and allow his head and neck to fall backwards. I then guided him through some relaxation breathing. As he began to let go, I slowly took his arms from his sides and raised them over his head. This slow action opens the heart and releases the tension in the chest. He was very relaxed at first, but became more agitated as his arms went higher and higher over his head. These muscles had been holding tension for a very long time. He said he felt he would have a heart attack if I didn't stop. The pain intensified around his chest. I closed my eyes to get a reading of his body. There was no indication he was in any danger. On the contrary, his body was calling for the release.

Bob kept insisting that I stop, that his heart was really in trouble. I calmly told him that he was fine, and that we would work just a little longer. "Keep breathing, I'm just going to move your arms up a little higher." He became frightened, but I don't think he wanted me to know, so he kept breathing and praying that he wouldn't have a heart attack. After about twenty minutes, which I'm sure to Bob seemed like an eternity, the muscles around his heart relaxed and let go. With this release, his chest area opened and he was able to get a full range of motion from his arms. He couldn't remember being able to move that freely before or having deep, full breathing easily available to him. The pain in his heart was gone, and he felt open and strong.

He later shared that as a child he had been very ill with a heart condition. One of his sisters died and as a result, his father had become overly protective of him. He told Bob that when he slept, he reminded him of his dead sister. He didn't want anything to happen to Bob, so consequently he never let him play with the other kids, or participate in school sports. Bob grew up guarding his heart. Over the years, the tension built. His father's fear literally encased his heart. But now it had been released. Bob left feeling lighter, younger and happier.

The following week, he arranged for me to talk to his group. As I entered the room, an undercurrent of defensive skepticism within the group was temporarily overcome by Bob's bubbling enthusiasm. After being introduced, I shared some of my experience and training. I talked about body readings and explained that the body has its own unique language, and that by learning this language we can understand ourselves and our bodies more fully. In turn, this can produce a happier, healthier state of being. I stated that the language of the body is very literal, and can often hold important clues to unlocking stored trauma and/or disease.

Everyone listened attentively, but I could tell by their faces they were becoming more skeptical instead of less. I knew that a demonstration would be the only way to reach them. I asked for a volunteer for a body reading. I was surprised when a hand immediately darted up. Liz was in her late thirties, New England bred, and the mother of two. I had not met her before this evening. I preferred not to know the person because readings seem more powerful when it is someone I do not know. Even a casual acquaintance tends to rationalize that I must have learned the information in some other way. I asked Liz to walk around the room several times, so I could study her gait and the way she carried herself. Then she stood in a relaxed position for a few minutes while I circled her. I did a condensed reading of about thirty minutes, although a normal reading in my office can be three times as long. As I overviewed her body and gave my interpretations, her facial expression turned from skepticism to awe. She stated that there was no way I could have known some of the things I had said. The rest of the group concurred, and I was invited into the fold.

Two weeks later I co-facilitated the group with Bob. After teaching together for several months, it became apparent that we both needed to develop different levels in this recovery in order to accommodate different issues that surface at specific stages. After months of hard work, we developed a three-level recovery process for adults who had been raised in alcoholic homes. This program was later expanded to include any adult raised in a dysfunctional home. The program was a huge success and commanded extensive press coverage, so much so that while teaching several groups a week, we developed a waiting list for months in advance. I was reeling.

It seemed that one minute I was struggling to make a living as a yoga therapist, while the next, I was busier than I could imagine as an ACOA counselor. Although yoga therapy played an integral role, it was not my primary work. Bob sent me private clients from his hospital work, and I started to see some group participants on an individual basis. In addition to the years we attended seminars for our own recovery, Bob and I went to many trainings offered for the professional. My life had shifted from slow motion to high gear. One day Bob suggested that I go back to school and get my degree. The thought of adding school to an already hectic schedule seemed crazy, so I shelved the idea.

I had been working on a book about recovering from childhood abuse, based in part on personal experience and what I had learned about healing. I was lucky to have an agent in New York who was willing to sell it. I sent off the manuscript and eagerly awaited the news. Although the market was flooded with inner child recovery books, I hoped mine would find a special niche. I was proud of the work, feeling it portrayed a balance between practical solutions and heartfelt compassion. My agent passed along letters from various editors at the major publishing houses. The problem, each said, was not with the writing or content itself, but with my lack of education. I would not be considered an authority until I had credentials to back it up.

The book had taken two years to write. Although discouraged and disappointed, it made one thing perfectly clear. I had to go back to school. I was determined to let nothing stand in my way. I had neither the money nor the time for school, but I knew I had to go. I remembered talking with Michael Lee during his yoga training about how he had obtained a Master's degree at Vermont College through their non-residential program. He was impressed with their program, and had suggested that I inquire about it at some point. That some point had come. I made arrangements to go to Montpelier for an interview.

The school was beautifully traditional with its brick architecture nestled in a picturesque New England town. I liked the staff, and the program certainly seemed do-able, even with my busy schedule. I could complete most of my studies at home and would only have to be in Vermont once a semester for ten days. Everything appeared workable except for the money issue. I filled out the financial aid applications.

Months passed as I waited to hear about reimbursement. I began to think about how I could accommodate school. I felt positive about finishing college and going on for a Master's, but when the rejection letters came in, my hopes were dashed. I was not eligible for any financial aid because they thought I earned too much money. I did not understand how this could be, since I lived alone and had to pay a mortgage and support a new business. I didn't know what to do. I had just enough money to go for one semester, and then I would be broke. I prayed for an answer, but none came. The only thing I could do was attend one semester and see what happened after that.

I had to trust that if I was meant to get the degree, the money would come from somewhere. I was willing to work, if the work would come. Another lesson in trust. If everything were laid out before us we would never need to develop a reliance on God. Instead, we would rely on what we knew.

I signed up for school, not even having enough money for books. I joked that that was what libraries were for. I made a commitment that I was going to finish school, and do the best I possibly could, without taking away from time dedicated to my clients. I would balance it evenly, and not try to do everything perfectly. I would give up the image of the straight A student, and happily settle for the best that I could be.

In the meantime, clients kept coming. Each semester I would mysteriously have just enough money to pay for school. When I look back through my bookkeeping records, I still can't figure out how I managed to do it. But I did, or more accurately, it was done for me.

The wonderful thing about being challenged to trust is that when you do, and are able to see the positive results, it is an amazing revelation. In those moments my perception is aligned with God's, and I know that no matter what challenges I may face, I am supported by a loving universe. In its simplest form, it is the absence of fear. Maybe that is the only challenge any of us face in a given lifetime: the choice between trust and fear. To which do we give the power of our beliefs? Which do we gravitate towards when our foundation is shaken? I had gone back and forth between the two like a ping-pong ball, feeling exhausted by the split within me. Now at last, I was beginning to see a shift. Prayer and meditation, yoga and yoga raining, and most of all my (then) seven years of abstinence from alcohol, had enabled me to feel more centered in trust, regardless of the external evidence. This shift allowed my body and mind to relax and let go in a way that it had never before felt safe to do.

Years ago when I first stopped drinking, someone said to me, "Now the war could be over." At the time, I didn't understand what they meant. Perhaps because for all outward appearance, the war may have ceased. But it was far from over within me. Now, after seven years of hard emotional work and soul searching I can finally declare a cease fire. With a deep sigh of relief and recognition, peacetime was here at last. Life took on a gentleness that I had never known before.

My dear friends Kenn and Chandra held a study group on the spiritual text, "A Course In Miracles." The Course felt as refreshing as a drink of pure, cool water after a lifetime in the desert. The words and message validated what I had known with such certainty as a child. The pain of the world had dulled my senses, and my knowing. Now, as I poured over the text and the workbook, I felt I had come home. I remembered the truth that had sustained me in my early childhood. I remembered the sweet angels that hovered over my bed on nights when my parents' drinking and fighting filled the house with a dark cloud of hate and despair. I would talk to them in the wee hours, after all the yelling had stopped, and finally fall asleep under their watchful gaze. How grateful I was to my dear friends for leading me back to my knowing through the Course. I did not know it then, but they would play an even bigger role in my spiritual unfoldment in the aftermath of my surrender.

My surrender came in the seventh year following my trip to Egypt, just as Ioch said it would. However, it did not come in the way that I anticipated. I envisioned, a path filled with clear lessons, and a resolute sense of where I was headed. I thought that my passage through the first five Obsidian Trials would markedly lessen my fear and deepen my understanding of each Trial. But in many ways, it did just the opposite. The more I came to understand each Trial, the more I became aware it was merely the tip of the iceberg. Each Trial consisted of many layers of challenges. Completing one challenge took you deeper towards the essence of the real lesson. As your understanding expands, another layer was revealed.

My revelation was that the Obsidian Trials were holographic. Each Trial contained the information of all the other Trials within it. This resulted in a great irony; the more I knew, the less I knew. At the same time, I realized there is really only one lesson to learn. The complexity of the lesson fragmented its appearance, and the human mind, in its need for order, divided it up into a number of lessons that it found more manageable. Through this awareness, I was brought back to the ancient Buddhist teaching of the Flower Garland Sutra of Indra's Net:

> In the heaven of Indra, there is said to be a network of pearls, so arranged that if you look at one you see all the others reflected in it. In the same way each object in the world is not merely itself but involves every other object and in fact is everything else.

The implications of this concept were profound. Not only were all the lessons contained in each other, but as the metaphor implies, all things were contained in each other. This concept of interdependence filled me with a deepening sense of purpose, and a relief from some of my fears. My heart was being lifted up and opened. I realized that by overcoming these challenges, I was accomplishing something not just for myself, but for everyone. By extension, every time any one of us overcomes our fears and mistrust, we score a victory for all the rest of us. I could see how the personal healing work that I had done so far, especially with the painful childhood abuse, was already helping others to heal.

Was it possible that these painful life lessons were not meant to defeat and hurt us at all, but were merely a personalized structure for being of service to others with the same struggles? If we do not take the responsibility to overcome life's challenges, then there is no benefit from the pains of life, and we are broken. In our woundedness, we pass on hopelessness and darkness, rather than the empowerment of light and true understanding.

A deepening faith and trust had grown within me. The communication lines, as it were, with the unseen world were opening up more and more, as it had in childhood. I began to feel God's grace in even the simplest moments of my life. I realized that release from these challenges was not merely the lessening of fear, but rather the positive expansion of trust. It is this expansion that eventually lifts the initiate up to the unified world of Truth. A world less bound by illusions, and unified in God's mission.

As my counseling practice grew and I continued working with people from different backgrounds - all of whom suffered from abusive childhoods - I began to see how my suffering led me to a place of compassion and understanding. This "gift", as I began to see it, formed a bond of trust between my client and myself, one that allowed the healing to come more easily. The most painful events of my life had been transformed into my most valuable asset. I felt as if I had crossed a bridge leading to understanding, compassion and forgiveness. I knew that a part of my work here on earth was to help others cross their bridges. True freedom was only possible with complete awareness. Even a trace of darkness would hold a person hostage. The prison of darkness had held me for thousands of years, and I was no longer willing to trade the grace of God for the temporary comfort of denial. A noble warrior now lived within me, and would not let darkness rob me of the light that I had worked so hard to behold.

I found working with others, although gratifying, took a tremendous amount of energy from my physical body. I knew that if I didn't take the time to replenish myself, I could lose my effectiveness, or worse, fall ill. I had to make a commitment to do my yoga work-outs and make monthly trips to my retreat cabin for rest and relaxation. These trips were becoming the most important aspect of my spiritual growth. In the past I had resisted and feared being alone, now it was a source of great joy. One such weekend, I headed up to the cabin as usual, looking forward to three days of silence and meditation. It was a cold, raw February day, and I was anxious to get there before dark. A stormy sky and rapidly dropping temperatures sped me on my way. As I pulled in to the parking area at the base of the mountain, I thought it odd that there were no other cars there. Although winter is not the most popular time of year for most retreatants, usually there were one or two hearty souls around. There were four cabins on the property spread out over hundreds of acres. A fifth cabin was inhabited by a rotational caretaker. Recently, a nice young woman named Gail had made the required one year commitment to serve. I couldn't imagine taking a whole year off to live on the mountain. Part of me thought it a wonderful idea, but the other part felt the loneliness would ultimately drive me crazy. I admired Gail's courage. We spoke only briefly at the beginning of my retreats as I checked in, but I looked forward to these meetings just the same.

With a knapsack on my back, I began the mile-long trek up the mountain. Clouds made the sky appear darker than it should have been, and a thick glaze of sheer ice had already formed on the mountain. Each step was slippery and I found it hard to walk. I was afraid of falling, especially with the extra weight of the pack. I started walking up the path sideways, digging with the side of my foot. It was laborious, and I wondered if I should turn around before things got worse. The wind began to blow an icy snow around which felt like needles hitting my face. I decided to turn and head back down. As I turned, I slid backwards and fell hard on my backside, sliding down until I hit a jagged rock. I felt some soreness as I used the rock to pull myself back upright. The wind was now howling like a bunch of hungry coyotes.

I could barely hear myself think. It felt more dangerous to head back down the hill because of the steepness. I was lucky the rock stopped my slide or I could have gone careening down much farther.

What should I do? Gathering my willpower, I adjusted my pack, took a deep breath and began the climb. Each step seemed more slippery and difficult to manage. I could feel the sweat beneath my coat, even though the temperature was now freezing. I did not have much farther to go, but I couldn't see too far ahead. I kept straining to find the light from the caretaker's cabin. I knew I could rest there awhile before heading off to mine. On beautiful days I would take a shortcut through the woods, but tonight I was staying right on the path. I finally reached the large suspended gong, which I sounded to let her know that I was on my way up. Her cabin was only perhaps 50 yards away, and I summoned up all my strength to get there. My face was frozen, and my eyes were more shut than opened because of the sleet. I could not see her light, but I knew where I was. I knew these woods from memory.

When I finally reached her cabin, a feeling of dread descended. There were no candles visible through the frosty windows, no smoke coming out of the chimney. How could this be? I feared something may have happened to her. I opened the cabin door slowly, hesitating at what I might find. I fumbled around until I could feel a book of matches and was able to light a candle. I called to her, but there was no reply, just the cries from the wind. "Please God," I prayed, "Do not let her be out in this storm."

I wrote a note to let her know I had arrived and would make my way to my cabin. I let my hands warm over the candle's flame, but I felt so numb it didn't make much difference. It was usually a ten-minute walk over to my cabin, and fortunately the path was relatively flat so I should be able to make good time. As I opened the cabin door, I felt my fatigue. Ten minutes would be a long haul under these conditions, but I had no choice. In hindsight, I probably should have stayed where I was, but at the time the thought never occurred to me.

Even though the path was along a ridge and fairly flat, it felt steep and endless. The rustic gate leading to my cabin was frozen shut so I had to walk around the wood pile, but the end was near. The cabin was only a few yards away but I could barely see it. My hands were so frozen I wasn't sure that I would be able to open the door. After struggling with both hands I was finally able to turn the knob. At last I was inside! I knew I could have easily died out there. Thank God for my little cabin!

There was enough wood inside to start a good fire. I would go out and get more once I warmed up. Usually I fetched a bucket of water from the well and carried it over on my way in, but that was not possible. I would just get some snow and melt it. A cup of tea would help to warm my inner core. I felt the chill surrounding my heart. I don't think I had ever been that cold. It was as if I were completely alone in the world. I felt little and insignificant, powerless under the lash of nature. I thanked God for my cabin, the warm stove, and the hot tea. Comforting warmth surrounded me as the snow piled high around my door. I would never leave for another week-end again without checking the weather report first. We can get so civilized that it is easy to forget how vulnerable we can be in the face of nature. I fell sleep holding my tea, too tired to even finish it. The birch wood crackled in the stove, and morning came in an instant.

I awoke to the sound of icy snow hitting the window from the force of the howling wind. The storm was still raging. Snow had piled up so high, I wasn't sure I could even get out the door. I put the last of the logs onto the warm embers before the fire died down completely. I would have to hurry up and dress if I hoped to get some wood and water before the storm got any worse. I pushed the door open. The icy wind almost blinded my eyes. I pulled my hood down over my face as far as it would go and headed for the outhouse. As I made my way through the snow, I thanked God for my long legs. I always joked that they were a yard long, an exact measurement. I needed all three feet and more just to walk in the deep snow. I moved the snow away from the out house door with my gloves. The window inside had blown open, depositing a nice little pile of snow on one side of the toilet seat.

I secured the window as best I could, and then made my way down the trail towards the well. There were no footprints anywhere, not even the deer were venturing out in this. Where was everyone? No chimney smoke could be seen except in the distance from my cabin. Was I here all alone? No one from back home knew I was on retreat.

I started to feel afraid, thinking about how stupid I had been. I didn't have a watch or a portable radio. The storm gave no indication of letting up, and I only had enough food for two days. Would I be able to get down the mountain tomorrow as I had planned? I could see Gail's cabin from the well, and there was still no sign of a fire in the chimney. She wasn't there. But she was always there. Had she gotten caught in the storm also? Perhaps she was hurt somewhere in the woods. I didn't know what to do. Should I try to find her, and if so, where would I start? There were miles of trails covering hundreds of acres. Even if I knew where to look, I don't think I could do it in this weather. It was a virtual white-out. It felt like I was in real trouble. Panic started to take over.

Fortunately, I stopped myself by staying in the moment and focusing on the task at hand. I started to talk firmly to myself. "You don't have time to panic. There is too much to be done. Get the water first." Even on a beautiful, sunny day the routine of filling the bucket at this well required a lot of coordination. Today it felt next to impossible, but it had to be done. The frozen bucket swung wildly in the wind, making it difficult to grasp with my wet, frozen gloves. My mind began to flash back on all the impossible tasks I had faced in the past, and all of them had one common denominator: I was left to handle them alone. I had always felt victimized by that fact, but today that feeling shifted. Perhaps it was meant to be for my highest learning. I had certainly learned self-reliance, but unfortunately along with that I also learned not to count on anyone. The pain of being disappointed was so deep that it was easier not to let anyone know what I needed. This false pride had been humbled in me over the years as circumstances forced me to reach out to others. Now the fury of nature was forcing my hand once again. I believed only the power of God could combat the forces of nature. Prayer seemed the only option.

I knelt down beside the well in the crusty snow, placing my cold, wet gloves together: "Dear Heavenly Father, I feel lost and powerless in the face of this storm. Surround me in your loving embrace and give me the courage and strength to do what needs to be done. Thy will, not mine, be done." I rose to my feet and began to drop the bucket into the frozen well. Miraculously, it landed perfectly on the bottom, and I was able to lift up a full bucket of water. The second drop into the well was the same. I knew that I was being helped by God's loving force.

"Thank-you, Father," I prayed. "How blessed I am to be able to feel your grace around me, to have you close and to know that I am loved. Nothing is more important than this, nothing fills my heart and lightens my load more than your presence."

Why do I struggle so with my own will when I know what is available to me if I will only invite it in? How can doubt and fear take hold of me when I have known the love of God so intimately? What happens to me that it slips so easily from memory?

Baffled, I began my journey back to the cabin. Interrupting the howling wind was Ioch's gentle reply, "Santi, you have opened to God's grace, but you have not given yourself to God. Your allegiance is still with your ego. That is why pain and despair always return to you. Surrender to God, turn your life over to his care, and innumerable blessings will flow. If you do it for love, you will never be without love again."

Ioch's words struck deep within my heart. I had been so hurt as a child that my trust had been shattered. Did I trust Ioch's words enough to give myself totally to God? Did I trust that I would never be without love again? I wrestled with these questions along with the wind and the snow, as I finally made my way back to the safety of my cabin.

Trust. Was that really the only issue? I spent most of my life alone, fiercely defending my independence to the point of isolation and loneliness. I remember so clearly when it began. I was about one-and-a-half years old and I was on the floor sucking my thumb. I don't remember what my mother was doing, but I remember my reaction to her. I looked at her and knew that I was much older than both my parents, and that they were not capable of taking care of me. What was worse was the knowledge that my mother did not have my best interests at heart, that I needed to grow up fast in order to take care of myself. Upon this realization, I took my thumb out of my mouth and never sucked it again. Since then, I wouldn't let anyone help me do anything, insisting I wanted to do it myself. Years later my sister expressed anger at me as a child because I wouldn't let her either help or play with me. I shut myself off in order to survive. I never had the common fantasy of wanting someone to take care of me. Actually, the thought repulsed me. It meant that I was needy, and I never wanted to feel that way.

This I now see was part of my wound, being ashamed of my needs, my humanness, my vulnerability. My mother was not able to give without resentment, and unfortunately, I inherited her disdain. Is that the unhealed part of me that is walled away from my beautiful Father? Is that the part that is afraid to let go and trust? Spiritual experiences have followed me all my life, and I am still afraid. I have always seen angels, and heard their loving voices. I have beheld the face of Jesus in times of great distress, Ioch's loving guidance is ever present, and still I am afraid.

How can this be? It is not as if I doubt that these visions are true and loving. My doubt and fear has never been in them, but rather stemmed from the wounds I endured in the physical world. My survival instincts were turned up to maximum, and I have been afraid to let down this wall of defense. None of my angels protected me from being physically and emotionally beaten for years on end. All of my prayers to be taken back to Heaven fell on deaf ears. I was not saved from being sexually abused. If I was not saved from the sick, perverted will of men, how then could I believe that I would be protected if I let down my armor? That was the real fear, that God was not my protector in this world. I had to be the protector here, so letting go was not safe.

I was now back at the cabin. The heat from the stove soothed my frozen face and hands. My clothes were soaked so I laid them out near the stove and changed into my warm, cuddly sweats. Watching the snow outside, I remembered a story I heard the teacher Ram Dass tell at a seminar. It was about General Napoleon who, upon visiting India, came across a Guru and was struck by the man's wisdom and peace. Napoleon wanted the Guru to return with him to Rome and serve as his personal sage. The Guru refused, stating he would not leave his homeland because God wanted him to stay amongst his people. Not used to being refused, Napoleon became angry and threatened to kill the Guru if he did not come with him. Much to Napoleon's surprise, the Guru burst out laughing, and said, with a fearless peace, "You can not kill me. You can kill my body, yes, but you do not have the power to kill me. So do what you will, but I will not leave India." Napoleon was so unsettled by the Guru's words that he fled immediately, leaving the Guru behind unharmed. This

Guru had already learned the lesson that I had before me. He was not attached to his body, but to God's will.

I began to cry with deep and grief-filled tears. What was the cause of this sobbing? My heart ached to the core. Life had hardened me, and God was asking that I be soft and open. Was I willing to give myself to God, regardless of what happened to my body? I thought of "A Course In Miracles" which defines a miracle as simply a shift in perception. I could certainly use a shift in perception now, because everything in me wanted to resist and deny this lesson. "Help me to see this differently, to understand the love in this lesson, for all I see is the fear." The Obsidian stone appears to be black, but on closer inspection one sees the iridescent light sparkling from within it.

This lesson is not dark, only my fear is dark. The lesson is for my freedom and my happiness. I am still attached to my pain, and my fear tells me that is what life is about. I can certainly have this if I want, but if I want peace and God and light, then I must relinquish those beliefs that contradict the will of God. When I am in my littleness, I feel so incapable, but when I am right-minded, I feel invincible and calm.

Exhausted from fighting the cold and wind, I fell asleep. The rest was deep and healing. I was awakened by a branch slamming against the window. The storm was still going full force as the snow continued to pile up against the door. I put on my outer clothes and went out to clear the entrance and fetch more wood. I felt as if I was the only person in the world, similar to the feeling I had in Egypt. All my comforts had been removed. There was nothing to distract from the lesson at hand. Here I was again, all alone and unable to leave. I went back to the cabin to make some rice. I doubled the portions and only ate a little of the tofu and vegetables, just in case I was stuck here another day. The rice filled my belly and helped warm me up.

I knew in my heart and mind what I must do. The real reason for being here and getting caught in this storm was because it was time to give my life to God, not half-heartedly, but completely and forever. My life was not meant to be mine. God, not I, was its true owner. He created me and has a plan that I cannot fulfill on my own. My fears, my inadequacies, are of no importance. What is important is God's will. "Thy Kingdom come, Thy will be done, on earth as it is in Heaven."

I went over to the cabin's altar and calmly lit the candles and some incense. Kneeling down with my hands on my heart, I prayed:

"This is the moment, Father, of my surrender. I am declaring my dependence on You. I gladly and joyfully give You all of me to do with as You will. Take my body, my mind, and my will, and use them for Your highest good. It is no longer important what Your will is but that I follow it absolutely. My feelings and fears no longer have value in any of my decisions. Your will decides for me from now on. I have known humiliation, pain and despair. I have had my heart broken by those that I held most dear. My body has been beaten and shamed to the point of becoming barren as a woman. I prayed for death, but death did not come. I have hardened my heart and hurt others in the wake of it, and now it is over. The war is over, the battle of my will has been lost and my armor no longer serves any purpose.

You are my Almighty God, my Creator and the bearer of all my gifts. You are the Guardian of my soul. I give You back what was always Yours. It did not belong to me and that foolish belief has caused me deep despair. I promise that from this day forward, my life is Yours. I will serve You for the rest of my days, and at the end I will hand You my soul. Thank you for leading me back to where I belong. All the pain and heartache was but an illusion. You are the truth and the light, and I am Yours."

I remained in silence for a long time afterwards. The grace of this surrender filled me with a quiet ecstacy that I did not want to disturb. I could have stayed there forever. The

the rest of my days, and at the end I will hand You my soul. Thank you for leading me back to where I belong. All the pain and heartache was but an illusion. You are the truth and the light, and I am Yours."

I remained in silence for a long time afterwards. The grace of this surrender filled me with a quiet ecstacy that I did not want to disturb. I could have stayed there forever. The burden of my ego had been lifted, and I could finally breath easily. My life was over, and God's life in me had begun.

Chapter Nine

The Twelfth Healer

I returned from my ordeal on the mountain unscathed, but inwardly a transformation had begun. I experienced subtle energy shifts and my dreams became more vivid and haunting. Powerful themes began to emerge, and I felt I was slowly being led into another realm of existence. At first my mind was not able to retain the images that captivated me in sleep. Oddly enough, I sensed this was the way it was meant to be until I was ready. But ready for what, I had no idea.

It felt as if two parts of me were operating at the same time. One part was unconscious and found this new dream experience mysterious and a little frightening. The other part knew on some level to trust what was happening. This part was centered and calm, almost satisfied, as if finally emerging from deep within to a place of light and recognition. The split between the two consciousnesses was in constant motion. At times the two realms seemed integrated and whole, while at others, they were a wide impassable chasm. Sometimes I wondered if this was what it felt like to be insane, powerlessly watching reality come and go. This new reality was beyond my everyday reality and difficult to grasp. It would become clear as the veil lifted and my surrender was put to the test.

Winter seemed endless, and the cold had its grip at my core. When I received a phone call from my dear friends Kenn and Chandra, with an invitation to visit them in Palm Beach, my heart danced. They were holding a seminar on A Course In Miracles and wanted me to assist them. Kenn and Chandra had just finished renovating an old Spanish house and casita, which meant I could have the guest cottage to myself. It was the perfect antidote for my frozen bones and agitated spirit. The weeks passed quickly and before I knew it, I was en route to the land of palm trees and balmy breezes.

It wasn't until I was already on the plane that I realized how isolated I had been. For the first time in months, I would be actively involved with a group of people. I became acutely aware how run-down my body and spirit had become. The trip to the airport sapped my remaining energy. I was glad the seminar would not be held for a couple of days so that I could rest. My mind was too tired to think, let alone espouse the merits of practicing personal growth.

Kenn and Chandra greeted me warmly. Observing my weary state, they led me through a beautiful garden path lush with tropical plants to my cozy casita. It was exactly what the doctor ordered. Chandra had filled the cupboards with herbal teas and evening chocolates. The nurturing atmosphere helped me let go and enjoy myself.

Some time after one of our long poolside talks, Chandra offered to perform a healing exercise on me. She practiced what is known as energy work and felt a session might do me some good. I had never had a healing done before, but coming from Chandra, I was certainly open to it. I trusted her completely and had heard from Kenn how effective the sessions could be. We arranged an appointment for the following afternoon when her healing room was cool and quiet.

It was a small room upstairs with a massage table. The minute I lay down I felt relieved. My body relaxed and my mind immediately slowed down. I closed my eyes and began to breathe slower and deeper. Chandra's hands moved in sweeping circular movements a few inches over my body. I became more relaxed. The cool breeze coming in through the open window gently caressed my cares away. As I started to drift off, I became aware that something was changing. Ever so gently, a lavender light filled my mind and body. My eyes were closed, but the light was clear and sharp. Along with this beautiful light came a deep sense of peace and joy. The curtain of time opened and I remembered that lavender light was given to me as my guiding light when still an initiate in Atlantis. Here it was again, flooding my consciousness with love.

My eyes filled with tears as this grace blessed me and I realized I was not alone. Through the opaque light, faint images of several large beings slowly appeared like wingless angels of enormous height. Although their faces were misty, some were discernibly male and others female. They formed a circle around me, benevolence beaming from their gentle smiles, filling me with inexpressible ecstasy. I realized these beings were my oldest and dearest friends and teachers, the ones I had been longing for my whole life.

I remembered as a child, looking up at my parents and telling them they were not my real family, that this was not my real home. My home was up there in the sky beyond the stars, and I would point to a star formation I later learned was called Sirius. I would lie out on the grass on warm summer evenings longing to be home, to be a part of my star family again.

Not until this moment did I understand who it was I so desperately missed. Here they were before me, eleven columns of translucent light, my Circle of Healers. I felt like a child in the presence of these great teachers. In my mind I felt them speak:

"This is a long awaited day, a great celebration for all of us! You are now ready to take your rightful place amongst the Circle of Healers."

They gestured to my place within the circle. "Now the circle is complete and the twelfth healer is finally in place. Dearest sister, we welcome you back. You have successfully completed the trials that have blocked your ability as a healer. The way is open once again and the gift is yours to share. We are here to train and assist you. Your initiation as a healer is complete, and all the Heavens sing with joy in this your victory."

I could not contain my emotion and began to weep from the altar of my soul. All these years of pent up loneliness and despair were released in their presence. Although we did not speak, Chandra was aware of what was happening. I don't think I could have said a word, even if I tried. Along with Chandra, the Circle of Healers lifted their arms towards the Heavens. As they did so, my energy body slowly rose up from the table. When it was about two feet above the table, it turned in a clockwise motion. As the energy became more intense, I began to spin faster and faster. It was a very bizarre sensation. My physical body was relaxed, feeling almost weighted down and immovable, while my energy body was spinning wildly around in circles. As a result, a vortex of tornado-like energy formed and passed in and out of my energy body in some sort of pattern. I was acutely aware that my energy body was being reprogrammed and elevated. It was like being electrocuted without any sensation of pain or fear. I was being altered and knew that I would never be the same again.

I was awakened by the gentle touch of Chandra who sat beside the healing table, her eyes closed with a peaceful smile upon her face. Unable to move or speak, I lay there for the longest time. I felt almost paralyzed yet at the same time rejuvenated and recharged. All I could do was smile at her as tears of joy ran down both our cheeks. How blessed I am, I thought. I finally understand why I am alive.

After a few minutes the excitement of what just happened welled up within. I breathlessly shared it with

Chandra. She, too, was aware of the Circle of Healers. They always appeared at her healings. Her experience was more one of sensing, whereas mine was quite visual. Yet we described them in exactly the same way, enormous beings of light whose presence filled the observer with a joy beyond words. How lucky I was to have been given such a powerful gift and share it with one of my dearest friends. Overflowing with energy, happiness, and sheer elation, I told her I had been initiated into the Circle as an apprentice. I was finally a healer again! Chandra shared my happiness, honored to have actively participated in this remarkable event.

Experience and truth are the purest of gifts, because they are a part of one's self. After years of silence and the fear of being judged for what I have experienced, the time has come to let go of that fear. My release from fear and silence is a yearning to share, a call that resonates deep within my being that will not let me peacefully hide within the shadows any longer. It calls to me, "This wisdom was not spoken for you, it was given to you. You are the carrier, not the receiver. It is not yours to covet."

My destiny holds the resolution of my karma, the joy that fills my heart and the peace that heals my soul. My ego's perception is self-seeking and therefore, will never support or fully understand my soul's journey. To expect it to would merely create conflict and doubt within and make the veil harder to penetrate.

As long as we are human we will have an ego, but we are not that ego, as the ego itself would have us believe. The elephant has a trunk, but it is not a trunk. The trunk is the elephant's tool for survival, but a tool without a master is useless. The trunk cannot survive on its own. Yet in the case of the ego, it believes that it not only can, but should. The ego wants control and it mightily resists relinquishing its power to God, even though by doing so it would gain true and lasting happiness. We must understand the nature of the ego so that we can control it rather than have it control us.

The ego has two basic operating dynamics. The first, born of fear, is the desire for complete control of its environment, people, places and things. Control enables the ego to experience the illusion of safety in the world. Secondly, the ego has an unyielding need to be right. When the ego-mind feels that it knows what is occurring and understands the way things function, it again experiences a sense of safety. This characteristic in and of itself is not bad and in and of itself is, if anything, an essential ingredient to survival. The problem arises in the ego's rigidity, which leads back to the original characteristic of control.

It is this two-fold dynamic that holds most of humankind captive and separated from its spiritual nature. If we feel superior or inferior about anything or anyone, we are in the ego. The ego's perception is dualistic, made up of good/bad, right/wrong, holy/evil, healthy/sick, and so on. It keeps us in a constant state of uncertainty and fear. Anxiety is a sign of ego-enmeshment. If we are in good health, we are relieved, but underlying that relief is the fear of sickness. If we are in love, we experience happiness, but is it not true that underneath that love is the fear of losing it, being betrayed or abandoned? There is no peace in the dualistic world of the ego, because if we have one thing, we are in fear of being visited by its mirror opposite.

This dynamic is similar to the trajectory of a ping pong ball flying back and forth across the net. One side is good, the other side bad. The ball goes back and forth, never stopping. It is just a matter of time before it travels back to the opposite side. Maybe our fear is really an intuitive knowing that nothing in the material world lasts and that change is constant. If it is viewed from a larger perspective, this awareness does not have to be fearful. By shifting our focus away from the day to day changes in the world, we can know the constancy and peace of God.

Prayer, meditation and an honest willingness to know God will reveal God. We are simply aligning with what is natural and truly powerful. What could be more natural for a spiritual being than a relationship with God? This is the path to empowerment, responsibility and service.

Ironically, the key to true humility is through embracing the enormity of who we really are. God is not meek, nor should we be. Understanding and taming the ego, and then becoming of one mind with the will of God, are the challenges in the fourth Obsidian Trial. The ego's personal will must be surrendered absolutely if we are to be lifted from the darkest aspect of our human nature. Letting go as demonstrated in this Trial is not a surrender but rather a recognition. It is the awareness that lights up within the mind of the individual when he or she understands that we cannot serve two masters, the ego and God. Service can only be to one. By attempting to serve both, we are cast into a wasteland of confusion where we tragically lose the benefits from either. Our struggle deepens and the load becomes unbearable. In such a state, life no longer seems worth the effort. In one way or another, we stop feeding life and, in turn, life stops feeding us. Eventually life, at least in the physical realm, is over.

When I decided to give my life to God in the cabin that snowy night, I committed myself to serving His will. It is only in retrospect that I understand this was only the first step in the Trial. The second step is the one that carries the light of understanding, and no Trial is complete without this light. When I saw the Circle of Healers, I understood there is a Divine plan for each one of us. We all play a unique role in healing the world's perceptions. It was not my life to give. It was the arrogance of my ego that believed it had anything that wasn't already God's. Ironically though, I had to completely surrender before I understood this. It seems strange that I wasn't able to see it then. But when the dawn comes, the darkness is immediately forgotten.

*   *   *   *   *

I returned home committed to the new direction that my life had taken. Along with Bob Cote, I continued to teach Adult Children of Alcoholics groups, whose popularity grew as people experienced the benefits of the program. I did not know how the healing work would manifest, but when the time came, I knew I would be guided.

I was pleasantly surprised that my first guidance would come in relationship to my best friend, Cindy. In my morning meditation I was told to call and invite her to come up for a healing on her throat. Cindy was a rock singer, scheduled to be in the studio for a recording that week. She was happy to get the call because she had come down with a sudden sore throat with only 48 hours to recuperate. I knew nothing of this until I relayed the information that I had received. She felt it was worth a try to come see me. I was a little nervous, never having done a healing before. I had to trust that although I didn't know what I was doing, I was confident the Circle of Healers did.

Cindy arrived feeling sicker than ever with great hopes that the healing would help. I must admit I didn't share her confidence and kept thinking how angry she would be for having driven all this way for nothing when she could have been in bed getting the rest she needed to recover. I reminded myself that I had to turn the whole thing over. I was not in charge. She lay down on the day bed in the healing room. I said a silent prayer for guidance, telling my Circle that we were ready as they had asked. A few minutes passed. Nothing happened. A few more minutes. Nothing. An eternity passed. Nothing. I kept trying to stay centered, but it became more difficult as time dragged on. "Where are they?" I thought to myself. They had told me to bring Cindy here and now they were nowhere to be found. I didn't know what to do. At least if I ended up looking like a fool, I thought, it would be in front of my best friend.

Just as I was about to tell Cindy I couldn't do it, something strange and unexpected happened. My arms slowly raised about two feet over Cindy's body and a tingling, spark-like sensation began in the palms of my hands. A minute or so later, silver sparkles began to emerge from the palms of my hands, dancing around like star dust and floating around her body. It was a beautiful sight. Cindy did not appear aware of what was going on. She continued to lie there resting, her eyes closed and her breathing slow and rhythmic. As quickly as it began, it ended. The Circle never appeared and not a word was spoken. All that remained were the sparkles tingling from the palms of my hands. When it was over, I sat next to my friend to see how she was. Although her throat didn't feel any better, she said she felt completely relaxed. She was still glad she had come and we had some lunch before she headed back.

Feeling so out of control was a hard adjustment to make. My personality was used to taking charge and making things happen. It was how I had always survived. But in the healing arena, I felt completely in the dark and impotent. Not a comfortable feeling, but clearly one that I needed to adjust to. The more that I experienced, the less I knew what was going on. At least my ego felt that way. My soul, however, had an opportunity to emerge and express itself, creating joy and satisfaction within me.

Two days after her recording, I received a call from Cindy. I could finally breathe a sigh of relief. Her voice had cleared up beautifully. She was thrilled by the way she sounded on the recording. Maybe the healing helped, or maybe it would have cleared up anyway. There was no way to know. I was just glad that my first healing was over.

Trust is always strengthened by venturing into the unknown, motivated by something that you believe in. If I were reassured ahead of time, if I had all the information beforehand, it would have been far too easy for my ego to take credit for the deeds and only find it necessary to trust in itself. I understood that I was meant to be kept uninformed. This provided an opportunity for me to develop my commitment and love to God in a tangible way. And I had to become willing to do so. I would later discover that this commitment is made up of ever expanding challenges in letting go. It never ends.

Developing trust in God, in truth, and in one's own abilities to fulfill the task that God asks of us, is the central characteristic necessary for overcoming the obstacles in the Obsidian Trials. Trust is at the core of all of the transcendent lessons. The power of trust successfully propels the individual through all the levels of initiation. Trust is demonstrated and strengthened through the continued practice and commitment of willingness, detachment and faith. It is the willingness to do God's will in relationship to that individual's mission (dharma) without reservation; the ability to detach from anyone or anything that does not support and/or contribute to the fulfillment of one's duty, and the daily dedication to prayer, meditation and devotion (faith).

Trust is not a desperate plea for help when a fearful situation grips us. It is the heartbeat of our soul, each moment sustaining and supporting us on our journey. There is no success, no transcendence without the characteristic of trust firmly embedded in one's character. Trust enhances and expands love. It therefore is the path that leads us to joy. Joy, unlike happiness, is everlasting because it is the result of the individual's soul aligning with the Grace of God. This alignment is the dance of intimacy between God and humankind which creates the reflection of Heaven here on earth.

My work continued to expand. Clients arrived from many different sources. I did not have to do anything to find new clients. It was simply a matter of remaining willing to serve and do what was necessary to stay centered and receptive to the healing forces. Everything else was being taken care of in a precise yet mysterious way. My mind, which loves to intellectualize, had to be slowly trained to accept those things in life which cannot be figured out. I was acutely aware what a waste of time and energy this form of thinking had been and how easily it could push me off track. I was being taught to trust the unseen and the unknown, to let go of the desire and need to question the how and why of things. Everything was going well and I felt myself letting go more and more as I witnessed the power that was being channeled through me.

Then came a guidance to go to the hospital and see John, a man I knew briefly who had been badly hurt in a motorcycle accident. He was in traction with several broken bones and a leg so badly severed in the crash the doctors weren't sure they could save it. Even with large doses of medication, he was still in a great deal of pain. I was told to go to him immediately and decided to ask Laura, a mutual friend of ours, to come with me. She knew I was going to perform a healing. I thought it might help John feel more comfortable if Laura were present. John worked as a car mechanic and was a very down-to-earth kind of guy. I was afraid he would think I was some sort of a weirdo and not let me work on him. Laura waited in the parking lot while I said a prayer. Before performing a healing, I always asked for help and guidance, for freedom from the bondage of my ego self so that I could become a clear channel. By the time we reached John's room, I felt centered and calm. The extent of his injuries were much worse than we had imagined. It was truly a miracle he was alive. He seemed surprised to see me but grateful for the company. I knew it was the right decision to bring Laura. Rather than beat around the bush, I told John directly that I was there to do a healing on him. He almost laughed out loud, but I think he reconsidered when he felt his broken ribs.

"That would be quite a big job, don't you think?" he said jokingly. "What do you mean a healing?" He was so funny it helped to lighten the whole situation.

I said I would work with his energy body which was a few inches above his physical body. I would maneuver the energy to help release the trauma from his physical body which would help him to heal. He looked at me as if I had two heads. It was obvious he didn't understand a word I said.

Then he looked at me with a long, sincere expression, "Do you really think this would help?"

I immediately replied, "Well, John, under the circumstances, it can't hurt."

Again he started to laugh and stopped himself, but Laura and I couldn't contain ourselves. I didn't mean to make light of such a serious matter, but it really was funny the way it came out. Taking a long look at all the apparatus holding his body together, he agreed.

"The pain is what I most need relief from. When it gets really bad, I wish I hadn't survived the crash."

I placed my hand on his forehead, "Let's see what we can do. At the very least, I think you will find this very relaxing."

I pulled the curtain around the bed for privacy. Laura sat in a chair at the foot of the bed while I stood alongside him. I asked him to close his eyes and simply ask for the willingness to receive the light of healing and help for his body, mind and spirit. I silently said a prayer for assistance and guidance. Almost instantly the energy began to move through my hands. In a matter of moments, John's energy body left his physical body and traveled high up above the earth. I could see him clearly in my mind's eye. We were able to communicate telepathically. This had never happened before in a healing and I wasn't sure how to proceed. I continued to pray but no information came, so I just trusted that it was all right. Several minutes passed. I could sense Laura was getting upset. I opened my eyes and looked towards her. She seemed relieved when I looked at her and asked if John was still breathing. I looked at John's body and noticed his breath had slowed down to such an extent that it was barely perceptible. I softly told Laura that it was okay and not to worry.

I closed my eyes again and asked John to come back into his body. Much to my surprise, he said "No. There is no pain now and I don't want to come back."

This really scared me. What had I done? What if I couldn't get him back into his body. Would he die? I prayed for my Circle to help show me what to do. As I focused in on their energy, my fear slowly began to subside. Then I knew that no matter what happened it would be all right. I was not the one who made him leave his body and I would not be the one to retrieve him. When I remembered my place, I felt safe. It is only when my ego got in the way and tried to control what it can't control that my fear skyrocketed. Calmly I let go and allowed the energy to move through me and into John's physical and energetic body. Slowly he began to descend into his physical body, his breathing getting stronger and stronger until he was fully present once again.

When I opened my eyes he was staring at me in amazement, "What just happened? That was the most incredible thing I ever experienced. I was high above the earth and yet I could talk to you and feel your presence. There was no pain, and I still can't feel any."

I reassured him that I was also aware of his experience, but that unfortunately his pain would return and that there was a long process of recovery ahead. Laura was dumbfounded but relieved when his breathing returned to normal again. After his initial burst of enthusiasm, John felt totally exhausted so we decided to leave and let him rest. On the surface I appeared calm, but inwardly I was pretty shaken up. My mind raced with questions and concerns. I knew I could not continue to do healings until I received validation from people I trusted in the healing profession. I could simply be delusional, which would certainly be dangerous to others and myself. I was certain that if I had the gift, other gifted people would see it in me, too. I needed reassurance in a tangible way, not just inwardly with my Circle and Ioch. If I really was gifted, I would gladly let it lead me, but if I was crazy, I needed to know so that I could get help and not hurt anyone.

My search began with a holy man from India, whom I heard speak years ago and who had returned to the states. I had been impressed by his unwillingness to accept any money and his total reliance on God to care for him. I hoped he might provide some insight into what I had experienced. The newspaper indicated he would be in upstate New York over the weekend and that private audiences were available. I phoned immediately and made an appointment. This was no coincidence. I knew I was being supported by the Universe to find the answers to my fears and concerns. I gave thanks and waited for my meeting on Saturday.

It had been almost a decade since my journey to Egypt. So much had happened and yet I still felt I was at the beginning of my journey, that I had only uncovered the tip of the iceberg. I had such a long way to go. Thank God for the support I received along the way.

Since Alma had given me "Initiation", I had read it several times along with Elisabeth Haich's other books on yoga and spirituality. Elisabeth had been the single most important teacher that I had over the last ten years even though I had never met her. The last book of hers that I read was "The Wisdom of the Tarot." I had resisted reading it for many years because I felt the Tarot had been misused and trivialized.

Gypsies used the expanded deck of 72 cards for fortune telling. The original greater Arcana cards consists of 21 cards and was used to demonstrate where a soul was on his or her journey in life. The cards denote levels of initiation and the lessons within that initiation. As I read Elisabeth's book, I realized this knowledge was within me as well. It simply needed to be reawakened.

I bought a deck of Arcana cards and began to read them. I did not follow the interpretations that came in the box. Rather, I let the cards themselves say what they meant.

Before long these cards stimulated my psychic abilities, allowing my inner sight to re-emerge. The Tarot cards unlocked a door within my psyche in which I could see the past, present and future. It also helped stimulate telepathic abilities that have lain dormant since Atlantis.

I could now hear and see Elisabeth Haich teaching me, not just through the words in her books, but on a personal level in my dream and waking states. It was similar to hearing Ioch's voice, but there was a difference that is not easy to describe. When Ioch spoke, I felt my ancient nature, young and naive, as I was in ancient Egypt. When Elisabeth spoke, I felt present in the moment, and the lesson at hand related to my current challenge. Her face clearly came to mind even though I had not yet seen a picture of her.

I wish I could say I understood everything in Elisabeth's books and teachings, but I am afraid I fall terribly short. There are sections in "Initiation" that continue to baffle me. I always prided myself on my intelligence and the speed at which I can learn and absorb most material. This was not the case with her teachings. Perhaps that is why she is here to assist me. In my prayers I asked for her help in seeing the truth and to be with me when I went to see the guru, Takar Singh.

Saturday finally came and I headed out to Columbia-Green College to have my private meeting with the guru. I arrived a little early so I could hear him speak on the topic of creativity. His peaceful manner had a calming effect and I knew I had come to the right place. There were several people ahead of me. I had to wait for over an hour, but somehow I didn't mind. It was interesting to watch people's transformation before and after their meeting with the guru. Some appeared to glow, while others emerged perplexed. Finally, I was next and this part of the wait seemed the longest. With only a few minutes to go, my mind started to blank. What would I say to him? How could I phrase my questions? Why hadn't I written my questions while I sat around waiting? I was annoyed with myself for being unprepared since I am usually so organized and clear. I couldn't understand why I was so spaced out. The door opened and it was my turn.

I walked into a large classroom filled with empty desks and chairs. Takar Singh sat at the far end of the room by a window. He greeted me with a warm smile. As I walked towards him, I prayed to be guided to the right questions and share what was important for him to know. While praying, I felt a shift occur. I actually felt liberated from any attachment to my mind. I told him of my struggle and of the amazing experiences that I had had, especially in the last year. My overall concern was whether I was experiencing some massive hallucination or the grace of God. I needed him to be honest with me. He gave a gentle reassuring smile and told me that it was indeed God's grace and that God demands we give our all. Anything less would be a lack of faith and considered as fear. He told me I needed to purify my body of all sugars by eating a simple diet and to depend on nothing but God.

He then asked me to look deep into his eyes. This request shifted my focus back to the moment, his black eyes penetrating my innermost being. I knew he could really see me. I was not afraid or ashamed. I wanted him to know who I was. That moment of recognition was punctuated by a bolt of white light that emerged from the center of his eyes and entered mine. My head went back as if I had been struck by lightning. I later learned the Indians call this gift from the guru shaktipat. It means the touch of grace. My session came to a close and I had to pull myself together so I could walk out of the room. It was a wonderful feeling, but very ungrounding to say the least. How would I ever drive back home?

As I rose to leave, he reassured me that I was not crazy. These gifts were God given and meant to be developed and shared. "Keep praying and meditating and let God lead you."

When I opened the door to leave, several people were still waiting in line along with his assistant who stared at me. The assistant seemed to know what had happened and congratulated me. I was moving in such slow motion that it felt like an eternity to get to my car in the parking lot. By the time I got inside, I was totally exhausted and fell asleep.

I had a restful dream about flying in which I tried to demonstrate to a group of people how simple it was to fly. No one in the village wanted to try and I could not understand why. Couldn't they see how much fun it was? What are they so afraid of anyway? Suddenly my dream was interrupted by a vision of Elisabeth Haich falling down some steep stone steps outside her home in Switzerland. I could feel that she was badly hurt.

I awoke with a clear head and drove home quickly. As soon as I got in I calculated what time it was in Switzerland because I wanted to call and see how she was. I had never called her before although I had taken the trouble to find her telephone number years ago. I picked up the phone and dialed, not allowing my rational mind the opportunity to talk me out of it. A man answered the phone speaking in English. It was her publisher. I introduced myself and explained that I was calling from the United States to see how Elisabeth was doing after her accident. He was noticeably surprised and asked how I could have possibly known of her fall. I told him of my vision and that although Elisabeth and I had never communicated before, we had communicated telepathically.

It seemed natural to speak honestly to him, but so out of character. Usually I am secretive about such things. He seemed at a loss for words because she had indeed recently fallen and broken her hip. The doctors thought it would be a slow recovery because of her advanced age of 93. He shared that she was most upset about having to stop teaching yoga at her school. Elisabeth called out from another room inquiring who it was on the phone. He asked who he should say was calling and for the first time since ancient Egypt, I used my soul name. "Tell her Santi is on the phone."

I could not hear what she said nor would I have been able to understand it. She spoke a combination of Swiss-French, German and Hungarian but no English. But I did hear a gleeful cry at the mention of my name. Her publisher said she was happy that I had called and asked if I could possibly come visit her in Switzerland. I was more excited than shocked by the invitation and without hesitation agreed. It was late fall and I always took time off at Christmas. I told him I would make the arrangements and would be there most likely between Christmas and New Year's. He relayed my message and we said goodbye.

I was reeling from the conversation. Switzerland! I had always loved Switzerland, especially Zurich, although I never knew why. I usually fell in love with places that were by the sea and Zurich was definitely land-locked, but I loved it just the same. I was so excited that I had to share the good news with my dear friend Lois. She was also a channeler and we had a deep spiritual connection. I knew she would understand without a lot of explanation. She was already aware of my connection with Elisabeth. As I related this amazing story, much to my surprise she wanted to accompany me on the trip. That's perfect, I thought. Then we could travel around the rest of the country and do some skiing and sightseeing. I had been to Europe before, but having a companion was certainly my preference, especially one who understood how important my meeting with Elisabeth was. Lois was interested in meeting her too. Over the year, I had often spoken of Elisabeth and she had read "Initiation". Naturally I could not guarantee a private meeting as Elisabeth was not well. We would have to see how it went once we got there. Lois understood the situation and still wanted to go, so we called our travel agent and made the arrangements. Once our plans were made, I quietly sat down to telepathically inform Elisabeth when I would be coming. I felt her presence receive my information and could also tell she was getting stronger, that her hip was healing nicely. Then in a clear voice, she communicated something that was a complete surprise:

"You are a fortress, the unattached defender of the Law of One. I stepped aside at your birth so that you could rule with Ptahstepenu, and I was there when you drew your last breath in the tomb after your fall from grace. Now a full circle has come to pass and once again you are faced with the lessons of fear. If you fail now, you may be lost forever. It is now time for us to meet face to face, mother and child, descendants of the Sons of God. Once again I pass the mantle on to you, to defend the Law of One by overcoming the darkness."

Her words were strong and resounded throughout my being. But most of all, it was her voice! She was the angel who comforted me as I lay dying in the tomb. She was the mother who died at my birth and gave me the magical amethyst stones to comfort and protect me as I grew up in Atlantis. Elisabeth was the beloved wife of Ptahstepenu, my noble father. I was overcome and remained motionless as I slowly assimilated this information and put together the fragmented pieces of thousands of years. It was all beginning to fall into place. I realized that I had always had powerful beings to watch over me. How silly, I thought, to ever feel afraid.

The night we were to board the plane for Switzerland was icy cold and I hoped the sleet would not delay our flight. We would be flying all night, due to arrive in Zurich at dawn. I never slept well on planes so I planned to read "Initiation" once more and write some questions on what I still did not understand. Lois was aware of my plan and seated herself a couple of aisles away so that she could sleep if she wanted. The flight took off on time and I soon became absorbed by my book. I heard Lois strike up a conversation with someone and they sounded like they were having a great time. After hours of their giggling, my curiosity got the best of me and I decided to investigate. Lois had met a nice man named Hans who hailed from Switzerland. He filled her in on all the best places to stay, where to eat and things we must do while visiting his country. I was thrilled because we hadn't made any plans other than to see Zurich and go skiing in St. Moritz. I was sure Hans' advice would help us avoid the more common tourist traps in one of the world's most expensive cities.

After a short visit, I excused myself and went back to my seat to continue reading. I don't think either of them missed me. I was happy Lois had met someone nice because I knew that I would be preoccupied for most of the trip. This past year had been a very hard one for Lois. Her father had died and the man she loved had broken off their relationship. This was her first trip to Europe and I wanted her to have a good time. It was nice to hear her laugh again.

I stayed fully immersed in my book until the captain announced we would be landing in a half hour. He pointed out we were currently flying over the Alps if we wanted to raise our window shades. The sun was just rising over the mountains and the snow glistened. How could anyone doubt that there was a God while witnessing such beauty and majesty? Our hotel was located on a quiet street across from a wonderful cathedral. Our room overlooked the church and we heard the bells ringing every morning. There was a beautiful arched window where we could sit and eat breakfast and two large feather beds that were large enough to get lost in. It was the perfect Swiss room in the perfect Swiss hotel. We both felt happy to be there.

That evening Elisabeth was going to teach and lead a meditation at her yoga school. We had planned to attend the session and then to meet with her privately the following afternoon. We spent the day shopping and seeing the sights. It was great fun and helped pass the time quickly. I was so anxious to see Elisabeth that anything that could distract me was welcome. Hans called and Lois decided to meet him the following evening. She wanted me to come along, but I wasn't sure how I would feel after my meeting with Elisabeth. I wanted to wait and see.

After dinner we made our way to the school which was only a few miles from our hotel. We got to the school a few minutes early so we were able to walk around a little before Elisabeth arrived. When Lois and I entered the meeting room I was pleasantly surprised to see the walls covered with all the original paintings of the Tarot cards that Elisabeth had adapted and designed. The paintings were striking, much more dramatic than the reproductions in her book. The room began to fill and everyone sat in a semicircle. We waited quietly for Elisabeth to arrive. When she entered the room, everyone stood up and smiled, sitting back down only after she was seated. She did not make eye contact with anyone. She simply rang a small bell that sat on a table next to her chair and closed her eyes to meditate. Everyone followed her lead. At first I was shocked by her appearance. I knew that she was ninety-three, but in my visions she came to me as a much younger woman. Her energy, though, was as I had experienced it, and I was thrilled to finally be in her physical presence. The meditation lasted about a half hour. She rang the small bell again and we opened our eyes. Elisabeth smiled at us and began to speak in German. Neither Lois nor I understood word but it really didn't matter. When the lecture ended, I hoped that Lois and I would at least have a chance to introduce ourselves, but Elisabeth disappeared too quickly. The man at the desk explained that she was still in a great deal of pain from the hip fracture and needed to rest as soon as the lesson was over. I was disappointed for Lois. I would at least get to meet her tomorrow.

The next morning we were greeted by a beautiful blue sky filled with singing birds. Breakfast consisted of lots of hot coffee, rolls, and cheese, and was delivered to our room. My fondness for Switzerland was growing. Lois preferred to eat in the downstairs dining room where she could meet and mingle with others staying at the hotel. An acting troop was staying in the hotel and Lois, having been in show business, was interested in connecting with them. I, however, was happy to eat my meal in the breakfast nook in our room watching people scurrying in the street below, and listening to the church bells. Today was the day I would meet my mother. My birthday was January 1, just a few days earlier and now I felt I would have another birthday.

I dressed after breakfast and went to find Lois. I had several hours before my meeting and didn't have the faintest idea how I should spend them. Lois was going to return to a few of the shops we had visited the day before, but I was interested in doing something different. I had always loved the Zurich zoo and made it a point to visit each time I came to the city. Lois wanted to stick to her original plans so we arranged to meet around five o'clock after I had my meeting with Elisabeth.

The tram up to the zoo was a wonderful ride, taking us past the Carl Jung Institute to the top of a hill that overlooks Lake Zurich. Elisabeth's house was just a short walk from the Institute and commanded the same extraordinary view. I decided to get off at this stop and slowly make my way to her house, allowing some extra time because I wasn't sure where it was. The zoo has one of the most amazing owl collections I have ever seen. I especially liked the ones that are about the size of the palm of your hand. The zoo wasn't crowded and I had plenty of time to pray and center myself before the meeting.

As I drew closer to Elisabeth's house, tears of gratitude welled up from deep inside. I reflected on the heartaches and blessings in this lifetime. I had been through so much and I was only thirty-nine. At ninety-three, Elisabeth was the reverse numbers of my age.

Her house was built on the side of a steep hill overlooking Lake Zurich. The neighborhood was quiet and unassuming although clearly upper middle class. I took a deep breath and rang the doorbell. Her secretary answered and fortunately she spoke some English. She led me into the living room and said that Miss Haich would be with me shortly. There was so much to see and study in this wonderful room. It was filled with beautiful art from all over the world but most pieces were from India. The most striking, however, was Elisabeth's painting of seven charging horses symbolic of the seven chakras, the energy centers of the body. It bore a resemblance to the painting that Rene had done.

Just then I heard Elisabeth enter the room. I turned and watched as she walked towards me with the help of her maid. She indicated that I sit down with her on the sofa. I was still not used to seeing her as an older woman. The woman who appeared in my visions was only in her mid- to late-forties. Elisabeth spoke in German. I told her I only spoke English and a little French. She spoke Swiss-French which is quite different from Parisian, but we were able to get by. I related my experience in the Great Pyramid and how my life in Atlantis was revealed to me so vividly. I told her I knew she had been my mother and that I still held her as such in my heart. She smiled and said if I ever needed her, all I had to do was think of her and help would be close by. She validated my gifts by telling me that I was a medium and a healer. I had brought my copy of "Initiation" with me and asked her countless questions. Elisabeth scolded me for ear marking the pages and writing in the book. She said books were sacred things and should be treated with great care and respect. When I asked her to write something in my book for me, she hesitated a moment, then jotted something down in German:

"Fur die liebe ist die liebe selbst der Lohn!"

I asked what it meant. She smiled and said, "It may take many years to understand, very few people ever do." Loosely translated she had written, "Love is the reward for loving."

"When we are in love," she explained, "if we are loved in return, then we are happy. But this is not love. The love is in the giving, not the receiving. Love grows within us and then we extend it out into the world. The more we share, the more it grows within us. The only way to lose love is to hoard it for fear that you will lose it. Love is free or it is not love."

She told me to go into the next room, a glassed-in porch that hung over the hillside because there was something there she thought I would want to see.

There on the wall was a full-length portrait of the younger Elisabeth, the one who came to me in my visions.

I asked why I had seen her this way rather than the way she was now. She smiled and threw her head back with a sigh. "You see, my child," she said, "we all hold an image of ourselves in our minds. That image is transported to others on a telepathic level. You see me as I am in this portrait because that is the way that I see myself. I am still shocked when I look in the mirror and see how old my body has grown, or when I attempt to achieve a yoga posture and can no longer do it with my body the way I see myself do it in my mind. I am still taken by surprise."

"Raja yoga," I said. "That is what you are speaking of, the yoga of the mind's eye. You see I have studied your books thoroughly."

"Yes, Santi, you are a good student. But it is time now for us to say goodbye. I am very tired. You know that you can speak to me as we have before whenever you need, and when my light goes out in this life you will know, but we will meet again on the other side."

She called her secretary to come in and help her to her room. My heart felt as if it were going to break. I loved her so much and knew she would be dying soon.

"Mother," I asked, "is there anything I need to know about what this life holds for me?"

She turned to me and said reassuringly, "You will know joy."

The rest of the trip was in sharp contrast to the experience of meeting and being with Elisabeth and yet it all seemed to flow together naturally. Lois and I took a train down to St. Moritz. The scenic views were dramatic and breathtaking. We enjoyed the ice sculpture festival, skating, horse shows and the magnificent countryside, everything a winter holiday could possibly offer except, perhaps, good skiing. Switzerland had very little snow that year and the skiing was icy and thin. Hans tracked us all over the country. I think it was healing for Lois to have an attractive suitor. The trip finally came to an end. Much of it was a fog because I had ben so preoccupied with my meeting with Elisabeth.

I was coming to realize that along with the validation of my spiritual gifts came a tremendous responsibility. I have always loved to travel and have fun and I have done a great deal of it in my life. But I needed to balance this with a serious commitment to my mission. I realized now more than ever that God had a plan for my life if I would just follow it. I hoped that Elisabeth's words were right, that the path would lead me to joy. After so much pain and heartache, what gift could be more desirable? The hope in my heart strengthened my resolve as another step along the way was taken.

Chapter Ten

The Reunion

My inner guidance had directed me to college, to graduate school for a degree in counseling psychology, and a thriving private practice in which I continued to minister to the very ill. The challenges I faced during this busy time included asking my guides for help and practicing trust.

When I began college, I did not know how I would pay my way. It was an instant replay of my undergraduate dilemma. I had just enough for the first semester, but after that I did not know where the money would come from. Since I had been guided to go back to school, I made a decision to trust that the money would be provided as long as I was willing to do my part, whatever that might be. However, it was a baffling dilemma. I worked a minimum of forty hours a week to pay my bills. School work itself required at least another twenty. My mind would spin when I tried to imagine how it would all work. There was the house mortgage, tuition and other school necessities, food and all of the other necessities of life. No matter how often I played with numbers or juggled hours in the day, I came up short on both.

I didn't particularly want to go back to school, but the guidance was strong and very clear on this matter. For reasons I did not understand at the time, it was essential that I get a Master's Degree, and perhaps my Ph.D. later on. Again, I was asked to exercise my trust in God. If this was meant to happen, the financial means would be provided and there would be time enough as long as God was guiding my priorities.

And as sure as dawn heralds the new day, funds came pouring in. I was so busy with my practice that I stopped accepting new clients. I had more than enough money to pay for my commitments. The one thing I did not have was time. I worked until six-thirty every night and then did schoolwork until one or two in the morning. Had it not been for the incredible inner support and love I received from my guides, I could not have kept up that hectic pace for as long as I did. There was nothing I could not do as long as I had their love and good wishes. The Circle of Healers were my closest friends, and I was grateful to have them. During those three years, most of my other friends gave up on me. I knew that the few who were able to understand and support me from a distance would remain friends forever.

Everything moved along nicely. I could clearly see the hand of grace in my life, but still something was missing - a life partner. Following my trip to Switzerland two years earlier, I was told by my guides that my soul-mate would join me on this mission at the start of the new decade. I was informed we would reunite during this lifetime to complete a mission begun a long time ago. I would recognize him by the blueness of his eyes. We would marry, honeymoon in Ireland, and be spiritually blessed by an old teacher who would remind us of our heritage. This blessing would protect our union and fortify us for the work ahead.

I nearly forgot about this guidance. The year 1990 was coming to a close, as was the new decade. Yet no one had shown up in my life. I began to doubt the message that had come to me. Perhaps it was just wishful thinking on my part and not a holy message at all. The mere thought of never meeting someone I could really love caused me a great deal of pain. I knew that I needed to turn this over to God.

I thought it might help to make a list of what was important to me in a mate and what I was no longer willing to accept. I knew I could not return to the dating scene, that no ordinary relationship would work for me. He would have to be a very special man, one who was dedicated to serving God and could understand and support my relationship with my Circle of Healers, for I was totally dedicated to them. As important as a man would be in my life, God and my Circle had to come first. I wanted a man that had placed his heart, as I had, on the altar of the most Holy.

I prayed for the willingness to accept His will in this matter whatever it may be and to guide me in the knowledge of it. As I prayed, my body relaxed and peace returned. I made one last request to my loving Father:

"Whether I am to have a partner or am meant to be alone forever, I will accept whatever Your will is for me, because I know Your will is always good, loving and abundant, regardless of how it may appear. But Father please, before I die, let me know love. Let me know the love that Elisabeth spoke of that expands beyond the perimeters of human understanding. Even if it is for a brief time, let me know it absolutely. I do not want to pass though another lifetime again without love."

A moment can feel like a lifetime and a lifetime can feel like a moment for one who has known love or the absence of it.

Ramanath or Michael Lee, the yoga therapist and founder of Phoenix Rising, was going to St. John in the Virgin Islands to teach with the Omega Institute. He suggested I join him to relax, eat lots of good vegetarian food, practice yoga, and recuperate from my rough schedule. The offer was too tempting to refuse and the price for the package was reasonable. There was no running hot water in Maho

Bay, but with everything else it had going for it, I thought I could survive.

Two other friends, Ron and Cheryl, wanted to go. The three of us planned to share a cabin and soak up lots of that wonderful Caribbean sun. The list of facilitators that were scheduled to attend along with Michael was impressive, but for the most part I was interested in connecting with Pat Rodegast, the channel for Emmanuel. Although I had seen her before, I had never spoken with her privately. I hoped there would be an opportunity on this trip.

Maho Bay lived up to all my expectations. The place was nothing short of paradise, even without hot water. We were perched atop a steep hillside overlooking the bay. Ron and I ended up sharing a cabin and Cheryl roomed with a woman in a cabin located a few feet below. Peacocks greeted us looking for a treat while banana birds sat along the railing of our deck and sang their sweet song. The paths to the cabins were actually raised decks so as not to harm this natural environment in any way. Cheryl and Ron were anxious to discuss the week's schedule, deciding which workshops they wanted to take. I opted to sun bathe, swim, and be as quiet as possible. I was so exhausted from my work schedule that even going dancing felt like too much work. I had the beach virtually to myself for several hours each day when classes were held. With every passing hour, I felt more refreshed and renewed. Ironically, as my body got stronger, my emotions became deeper and more painful.

A few weeks earlier, I had celebrated my fortieth birthday with a large group of friends who showered me with a wonderful party and beautiful gifts. Although I have always been blessed with good friends, my heart suffered from the absence of someone special. With each passing year, my loneliness became more unbearable. I knew I was attractive and could certainly be in a relationship if I wanted, but I was no longer able to settle for just physical companionship. I wanted a peer, someone who was an equal on all levels of consciousness, but this type of relationship had always eluded me. Where was my partner? Did he even exist?

I was walking up the stairs from the beach to my cabin when I ran into Pat Rodegast. She was headed to the beach for her daily swim and I asked if we could talk for a few minutes. She said she remembered me from one of her talks in New York and was happy to chat. Since she had developed the gift of channeling after she married and had children, I thought she would understand some of what I was going through. I shared with her my doubts and fears, relating how I had been given the gift of healing, which was joyous but also isolating. She understood my situation and was generous and honest in her own sharing. She, too, was sometimes plagued with doubts and inner struggles. Just knowing that I was not alone lightened my load. I thanked her and went back to my cabin.

I had scheduled a massage for that afternoon, and the timing could not have been more perfect. The masseuse arrived with her massage table on her back and asked if I wanted the massage on the deck overlooking the ocean. I welcomed the idea wholeheartedly and laid down on the table. It was one of the best massages I ever had. My body relaxed in a way that it had not in years.

After she left I took a long nap on the deck, waking just in time to prepare for dinner. I dressed quickly and headed down to the patio to meet Ron and Cheryl. Much to my surprise, I bumped into Pat again. She was glad to see me because she needed my help. She had just come back from sailing on her friend's boat and had told him about me. Her friend had a strange rash all over his body that particularly affected his hands which were severely cracked and bleeding, making it hard for him to sail. He owned a charter business out of Tortolla and was afraid that if it didn't clear up, he would not be able to work. She told him I was a healer, and that maybe I would work on him. My first reaction was dread. I was already so drained I felt I had nothing to give.

A second fear came straight from my ego. What if I worked on him and nothing happened? Fortunately, the other part of my mind was able to kick in, immediately reminding me that the results of a healing are none of my business. My job is simply to say yes and channel the energy. I told Pat I would be happy to do what I could. We made arrangements for her friend to come to my cabin the following afternoon.

I spent the day swimming and enjoying the sun. About an hour before the appointment, I cleaned the cabin, prayed and meditated. By the time Ted arrived, I was in a very clear, calm space. The minute he walked in the door I received information as to the nature of his condition. I took his nearly disfigured hands into mine and was filled with a flood of knowing. We spoke for about a half hour. I shared my vision of his unhealed past which I knew had caused this painful rash. I then did some energy work on him which his body responded to immediately. We made arrangements to meet the next day to motor boat over to a small deserted island nearby to do some energy releasing work using sound. I thought he would be less self-conscious if we were in a place where no one could hear us.

I met Ted on the beach the next day and already his hands were beginning to clear up. This, he felt, was miraculous but even more so was the fact that he was free from physical pain for the first time in almost a year. He had been going to doctors for months getting creams and medicines, yet nothing had helped even in the slightest way until now. I was happy for him, and realized that God in his Divine wisdom gave Ted this sign so that he would be willing to release these toxic energies from his body. We spent about a hour on the island sounding and releasing energy. It was exhilarating and exhausting for us both.

When he brought me back to the beach on the boat I didn't know how I would summon the energy to climb all those steps back to my cabin. When I finally got there, I fell right to sleep. Again, I awoke just in time to get ready for dinner. By the time I made it down to the dining area, however, everyone had already begun their meal. I got my food tray and made my way over to our table. The dining room was all a-buzz, and I felt people staring at me. I saw Pat who called me to a table she shared with Michael. She was pleased that Ted was having a remarkable recovery. His hands were almost healing right before his eyes. In his excitement, he had told everyone I was indeed a very gifted healer.

I felt happy for Ted, but mortified that he had talked about me. I had come on this vacation for some quiet rest, not to have a lot of attention focused on me. Secretly I wished to be invisible. A lesson I needed to learn was how to give and be of service and accept being sought after, while personally I felt isolated and alone.

Ted continued to heal and glow with the absence of pain, and I thanked my Circle for guiding me and showing me their profound abilities. The last days of the trip were relatively quiet. I had time to reconcile, at least in part, some of the conflict within me. Pat was reassuring and said that when it was time to meet my partner, nothing would stand in the way. I jokingly said to her and to God, "Well, he will have to come to my office because I am too busy and too tired to go looking for him." The joke was on me, for that is exactly what happened only a couple of weeks after my return from Maho Bay.

Back in the Berkshires, I resumed my busy work schedule. Before the trip a colleague named Ann had referred a friend who had some subtle health issues that he was trying to resolve. He had been to all kinds of healers over the years, but no one had been able to pinpoint the root of his occasional cardiac and bronchial problems. Ann suggested that yoga therapy might work for him. He resisted calling me for about a year, but finally her constant urging forced him to make the call. We had talked briefly before my trip to Maho Bay and we made an appointment for when I returned. Today was the day and I looked forward to meeting him. I had no particular feelings about the visit other than this was an old friend of Ann's whom I hoped I could help in some way. I was more than pleasantly surprised when he walked in the door.

It was one of those bright, sunny winter days when everything sparkles and feels brand new. Chris entered my office with a big smile and a firm hand shake. I could tell by his puzzled look that I wasn't what he expected either. I later found out he had pictured me as short, muscular and athletic with closely cropped hair, a description that could not be further from my real appearance.

As we greeted each other, all I could see were his crystal-clear, Atlantean blue eyes. They were the exact color of the sea surrounding my beloved home from long ago. Just seeing that color flooded my mind with fond memories and made me feel homesick. My momentary distraction was corrected when we made our way over to the deck to sit and fill out a standard client form. We reviewed the information and I realized that although he appeared to be strong and in good athletic condition, he had several underlying conditions that indicated congested energy. We both agreed to begin the process with a general body reading, the technique I used for gathering information from the body's bones and muscles to determine what the body is communicating. For example, if someone carries a lot of tension in their neck and shoulders, this could indicate the person feels over-burdened or has an over-developed sense of responsibility and a need to be perfect. Each area of the body is studied and this information is then brought together for analysis.

Chris had so many different, subtle body conditions we both felt that the reading would be informative and a good place to start. It took about an hour and a half. I recorded my findings as I went along. I told him to go home and listen to the tape at his leisure, assimilate the information slowly, and write down any questions that he might have for our next meeting. We made an appointment for two weeks later to begin yoga therapy on his lungs.

When Chris left I missed his presence. Although I did not have time to dwell on that feeling, I found it odd. Two weeks later, he came back and again I was immediately drawn to his blue eyes. I asked him to bring along some sweats for the session because we would be working on the floor and he needed to be comfortable and able to move around easily. While he went to change, I stretched and limbered up. When he returned we did some basic warm-up exercises to relax his muscles. Then I asked him to lie on the floor on his belly. I wanted to work at opening his heart and lung area by holding his arms behind his back and raising his trunk off the floor, a posture called the assisted cobra. The cobra position forces the chest to open and lean forward as the back arches. The affirmation associated with this position is strength through vulnerability.

I asked Chris to inhale taking deep, even breaths while allowing me to support his body. The more the client allows the therapist to do the work, the more the muscles and the deep holding can begin to be released. This process often feels good for the muscles, but can bring up a lot of old, stored-up emotions that are not always welcomed or understood. I could tell by the way Chris' breathing began to change that there was, in fact, some opening taking place. What I did not expect, however, was that there would be some opening taking place in me too. Images of Egypt flashed before me and Tenu's golden, glowing face kept coming into view. I tried to center my mind back in the moment, but it kept slipping away.

Chris was ready to rest, having opened more in the session than he thought he would. He had a lot of emotion coming up. I could tell that he just wanted to end the session and be alone. We made another appointment and before I could blink an eye, he was out the door. The door closed and through the glass, I saw him climb the outside stairs that led to the driveway.

As I watched him, I experienced another flashback to Egypt. This time I was watching Tenu turn and walk up the stairs of the Temple of Heaven with the Secret Tenets. That was the last time that I saw him until today. His words came to mind, "Santi, we will meet again for the final lesson and you will know me by my eyes." This was Tenu, my dear friend Tenu! I wondered if Chris was aware of our past also. My heart flooded with love for Tenu as the awareness of our reunion deepened. We were finally reunited and I knew that my life would never be the same again.

My mind raced with speculations as to what destiny held in store for Chris and me. Was he thinking of me, was love flooding his heart as it was mine? I knew that we were partners in a mission that had begun a long time ago. What I didn't know was what I was supposed to do next.

The day of our next appointment, a colleague invited me to her birthday celebration. I naturally accepted and then it occurred to me this might be something Chris would like to do because there would be several mutual friends at the party. When we finished our session, I asked if he would like to go with me that evening. He immediately said yes.

This began our dating phase. I wish I could say it was love at first sight and everything went smoothly from that day forward, but nothing would be further from the truth. It seemed the more that we saw of each other, the more resistant and distant Chris became. I was confused by the mixed messages. My inner guidance assured me this wall between us was temporary, and no matter how much Chris protested and insisted he didn't want to be involved in a serious relationship, I should just ignore him and continue to be available and open. This was easier said than done. On a good day, I was able to turn the whole thing over to God; on a bad day, my ego would kick in and I wondered why I tried to be involved with someone who kept saying he did not want to be in a relationship with me or anyone else. I recall at least a dozen times I threw in the towel, convinced that my guidance had been wrong. Although I never doubted that he was Tenu, perhaps he and I were not meant to be together in this lifetime after all.

This turmoil continued for about six months until an interesting shift happened. Chris and I and a group of friends rented a house in Rhode Island on the island where I was born. We were to be there for a week to enjoy the ocean and the fresh seafood. I always felt at home by the sea, and this island was a very special place. I had rented the house for several summers. It was lovely as ever, except that a mild hurricane had struck the week before and the beaches were still officially closed. This eliminated most of the tourist crowd and the island was unusually quiet and beautiful, very much like it was when I was a young girl. The beaches were ful of seaweed and debris, but were perfect for swimming. It was as if we had our own little resort to ourselves.

This quiet beauty and solitude turned out to be the perfect atmosphere for Chris and me to finally bond and fall in love. In retrospect, much of his resistance to being in this relationship was the inner knowing that it would not be a minor or simple affair. He felt he had already been through enough with his past loves. One morning after a particularly powerful evening together, Chris and I sat at the dining room table having breakfast, our throats tight with what we each were trying to tell the other. Chris succeeded in speaking first, his words aligned with my knowing, "You know that we are meant to be married, to be partners in love and in work." I nodded and he took my hand. I could feel the truth and the fear that we each had in facing this realization. Each of us knew in our hearts that this was to be a marriage of joy, challenge and service. We knelt together and prayed to be up to the task that lay before us.

From the moment we acknowledged the true nature of our relationship, life seemed to move at an accelerated pace.

Before we knew it, we were sitting down to pick the date for our wedding. Work schedules and the long Berkshire winters helped us arrive at a March wedding date. Then there was the question of our honeymoon. I was adamant that we take a two-week vacation. After our tumultuous courtship, we needed the honeymoon to recuperate. Both of us loved the Caribbean so we began to plan a relaxing vacation there. Suddenly a strong feeling came over me. I remembered receiving guidance many years earlier indicating I was to honeymoon in the British Isles. I mentioned this to Chris and immediately got out my box of old journals to try and find the reference for more details. Almost simultaneously Chris remembered a similar guidance that he had gotten from a psychic in Vermont a few years earlier that said the same thing. Then he began rummaging through his boxes of old tapes to try and find his reading. Both of us eventually found what we were looking for and, to our amazement, the information from these two different sources was exactly the same. We were to honeymoon in Ireland where we would meet a holy man who would remind us of our heritage and bless our vows.

This mutual guidance helped strengthen our commitment to one another and follow the word of God, regardless of the form it might take. We canceled our plans for fun and sun in the Virgin Islands and made arrangements to go to England, Wales and Ireland where we would visit the sacred sights, castles and cathedrals. As each day passed, it became apparent that Chris and I were on a path that had been laid out by mighty hands. All the dreams of a soul mate that I had held in my heart since childhood were now finally coming to pass in my fortieth year of life.

Our wedding was held at an old inn. My best friend Cindy wrote a song for the occasion called "All of My Angels," and Chris surprised me by playing "Amazing Grace" on the bagpipes. We were blissfully high on love and friendship and headed off to Boston to catch a plane to

London. I had been to London several times and couldn't wait to show Chris my favorite sights, most especially, the Tower of London. We managed to pack about a week's worth of sightseeing into a couple of days.

Our itinerary was tight because there were so many places that we wanted to see. From London we went to Bath, took a train through Wales, and caught a ferry to Ireland where we rented a car and drove to the Cliffs of Moher. I had wanted to see them since I was a little girl. We drove madly trying to get there before dark and arrived at the cliffs in a fierce wind and rain storm so powerful that it was easier to crawl than to try to walk against the force of the wind.

A dense fog covered the area. We had no idea how high up we were or how close to the cliffs' edge. The thunderous roar of the sea sounded far below, but no amount of imagination could have prepared us for what we were about to see. Despite my screaming protests, Chris got up on the ledge, trying to get a glimpse of the ocean. Then he decided to make his way over to O'Brien's Tower about 150 feet up the path. This might not seem like a long way, but crawling and holding onto the large boulders along side the path was a slow and tedious way to travel. He insisted I follow behind him, which I did reluctantly. The force of the wind was so great that the few wisps of hair that escaped from my scarf felt like little needles piercing my face.

We finally reached a stone bridge where the sea shot up into the air like a geyser. In order to cross the bridge and get to the tower, we had to push our way through this stream. I absolutely refused to go further and didn't want him to either. I was afraid he would be sucked right up and off the cliff. Chris had no idea how high up we were. When I told him we were 700 feet up, I don't think he believed me. He kept trying to get me to cross and I kept trying to get him to come back. We were at a stand-off. It became apparent that this man was even more stubborn than I. If we were ever going to get out of the rain, I'd better go along with him.

As I made my decision, Chris stood on the cliff. The clouds below suddenly opened up ever so slightly and he could see the magnificent view. His face showed that he was awed by what he saw. I made my way to him as best I could. Then I too saw the splendor of this place. It was as though we were the only two people in the world, facing the beauty and power of nature. The seas swelled over thirty feet. The stream of water we had passed was being sucked up the side of the cliff for over 700 feet. The cliffs in the distance kept ducking in and out of the wind and fog. We held each other, laughing with tears of joy at the exhilarating and purifying experience that was all around and through us. Ireland was our homeland and we were bathed in her splendor.

As darkness descended, we made our way back to the car. We had planned to stay at a bed and breakfast in Galway that Chris' coworker had recommended. After an hour of driving through the storm in clothes soaked to the skin, we came upon a small village. A crowd of people were coming out of a church and another, slightly larger crowd were headed towards a pub. We saw a small family-type restaurant that looked open. Wet and hungry as we were, we ducked inside.

Chris got our dry clothes from the trunk and as he went in to change, I ordered dinner. My hair was so wet it literally formed a puddle on the table. I thought it best not to sit down in the chair until after I changed. The waitress was sweet and understanding, which is how we experienced most of the Irish people. When I came out of the ladies room drier, the restaurant began to fill up. The rainstorm was still very heavy. Most patrons entering the restaurant were nearly as wet as we had been. We were the only ones that changed clothes while waiting for dinner.

The meal was delicious and filling. I hoped we would have the energy to make it to our hotel, still several hours away. As we made our way through the back roads of County Clare in the wee hours of the night, I was struck by how much had happened to us since we had arrived and couldn't imagine what else this wonderful place had in store.

Galway was beautiful and rich in history, but we were anxious to get to Dublin so we left right after breakfast. The countryside dotted with sheep was exactly what we had expected. Even the old abbey that had been converted into a hotel where we had lunch was somehow predictably perfect.

After a while the vivid scenery faded into the background and all we could focus on was how far we were from the city. It took much longer than any of our maps indicated, something we learned to adjust to on our trip, but we managed to arrive by late afternoon, giving us some time to sightsee before dinner. Our hotel was beautiful. Located in the heart of the city, we could walk to a number of sights. But after walking awhile, our energy plummeted and we decided to go back to the hotel, eat dinner and make it an early night.

We were pleased to learn we could use a health club located in another hotel as part of our stay there. Having lugged our heavy bags for almost two weeks, the thought of a swim and a hot sauna couldn't be passed up. No matter what else we did the next day, we would make it a point to get to that club. Monday dawned bright and sunny. We left the hotel early and walked up to St. Steven's Park. We decided to part for a few hours. There was a church I wanted to visit and Chris had some secret plan up his sleeve.

We met for lunch at a cute little place called "Fitzers" where Chris told me he had a surprise for me. We finished eating and grabbed a cab. Chris gave the cab driver a piece of paper with the address of our destination. It was all very mysterious and fun. We crossed a bridge by St. Patrick's Cathedral and appeared to be leaving town when suddenly the cab pulled abruptly over to the curb in front of the walls of Collins' Barracks (the oldest active duty military barracks in Europe). I gave Chris a puzzled looked. He smiled and paid the driver.

We walked to the entry gate where a sentry, who apparently was expecting us, led us to a reception room inside the gate. No matter how I tried to pry it out of him, Chris would not say a word. We waited a few minutes before the sound of precision footsteps could be heard approaching from down the hall. The door opened and there before us stood a tall, straight-backed sergeant wearing a green beret and fatigues. He addressed Chris formally and asked us to follow him. He walked us briskly all the way to the back of the building and out to a cement courtyard with high walls where several men waited in formation, holding bagpipes and drums. He directed us to sit on a low wall and politely asked if there was anything in particular that we would like them to play.

We were being treated to a private concert from the world famous Irish Army Pipes and Drums! I looked at Chris in amazement, unable to imagine how he had ever arranged such a thing. At Chris' request, they played one of his favorites, "The Dark Island," and several other tunes, in a way that I had never heard the bagpipes played before. Then Sergeant Byrne invited Chris to play something with the band. One of the men offered his pipes and suggested they play "Amazing Grace," which they did, just for me. I was touched and filled with joy. It was a moment that I know Chris and I will never forget. We thanked them from the bottom of our hearts and left to walk over to St. Patrick's Cathedral.

Because it was a Monday afternoon in off-season, the church was empty. We were able to pray and meditate without distraction. We were both overwhelmed with feelings and at the same time experienced a deep sense of renewal. The Cliffs of Moher, the concert and now the church were powerful, purifying experiences. Little did we know that they were all part of an elaborate preparation that would culminate later that evening.

We took a cab back to the hotel. While we enjoyed a hot cup of Irish tea, we both decided simultaneously to head over to the health club before dressing for dinner. It was only a few blocks away but we were feeling pretty exhausted, so we took a cab. If we felt sufficiently renewed, we would walk back. The hotel that housed the club was a five-star hotel and ours was only a four. The difference was visible. The club was modern, although the pool seemed more designed for treading water than lap swimming.

Just as we were ready to enter the sauna, a very large, overweight man went in. We knew there would be no room for us in such a small space. We assumed he wouldn't be long. Our sore limbs encouraged us to stay in the pool a little longer and wait for him to leave. I was becoming impatient when, to our surprise, a waiter entered the pool area carrying a silver tray of scones and coddled cream, which he delivered to the man in the sauna. Chris and I looked at each other in amazement. This distracted us from noticing that a tall, silver-haired priest had entered the area. We caught a glimpse of him as he went into the men's locker room to change.

We had given up hope of ever getting into that sauna and had gotten out of the pool, planning to shower and dress, when the fat man emerged, grinning with enjoyment and waddled towards the men's locker room. We quickly ran to the sauna before anything else could happen and started to relax. It was very hot, just what we needed.

Our bodies were soaking up the heat as the door opened and the priest we had seen, now in a bathing suit, came in and joined us. He was silent at first, except for the polite greetings upon entering. But he kept glancing my way, as if trying to place me. Finally, he apologized for the impropriety but stated he could not help staring because I reminded him of a girl he had grown up with and had planned to marry before he answered the call to the priesthood. He had been a journalist turned lawyer turned priest.

Obviously a brilliant and interesting man, he went on to tell us a riveting history of the dawn of Christianity in ancient Ireland, the history of Ireland and the lineage of his family. His people were from the Aran Islands in the mouth of Galway Bay. He was a wonderful storyteller and had us totally enthralled except for our mutual awareness of how hot the sauna was getting. I thought I was going to pass out, but I knew, as did Chris, that we were meant to stay there until he had finished with us. We both had the feeling that this was an important moment, an initiation of sorts.

He spoke brilliantly for about thirty minutes, when he began to describe a book that he had been working on for over ten years on the meaning of love. When the discussion turned to the subject of love, I interrupted to tell him that Chris and I were on our honeymoon. Visibly delighted, he congratulated us at length and then earnestly asked if he could give us his blessing. How could we decline! We stood up, bowed our heads, and received Father Powell's blessing in the traditional Latin.

Words cannot describe the powerful gift that he gave us. This was our blessing from the holy man, our "blessing in the sauna." We realized then that we had been led and prepared for this gift, that the heavens smiled down upon our union. My prayer to know love before I died had been answered a thousand fold and I knew that there was a plan for each one of us here on this planet; that God's grace was available for anyone who opened to receive it. We met with Father Powell once more before we left Dublin and our friendship and bond was established. Even if we never meet again, he will always be our holy man, and his blessing our strength.

We returned from Europe validated and committed to the work we must do. We established the Galactica Institute for Human Development and began teaching workshops together on a large scale. In addition to my psychotherapy and my work with dysfunctional family members, we now addressed the area of personal empowerment. I helped people deal with the challenges of the Obsidian Trials that they, too, were facing. But at this point, I incorporated them into traditional psychotherapy because it seemed effective. I realized that I was still not ready to put the teachings that I had been given out into the world in a direct way. In retrospect, I saw that until I fulfilled all the elements of the lessons, I was not qualified to teach them.

Chris had over twenty years' experience teaching meditation to individuals and corporations in addition to his regular work. He had begun his journey with the Maharishi in the late sixties and spent several years studying with him and becoming a qualified teacher himself. During the 1970s, he traveled with this organization and taught meditation all across the country and in Europe. He established a meditation training program at Galactica which turned out to be a powerful healing tool for many of my clients. Galactica continued to expand and Chris and I grew closer. Not all the details of our mission together were clear, but the foundation had been set and the path was beginning to emerge. It was by far the happiest time in my life.

Chapter Eleven

The Final Lesson

I think that God in His Grace does not let us see too far ahead on our journey through life. He twists and turns the path to prevent the long view. The seventh and final Obsidian Trial was around the next turn and I, in the happiness of my new marriage, did not see its approach.

Not long after our return from Europe, we were given an opportunity to buy a charming old farmhouse in the neighboring town. It could not have been more perfect, with an old barn and a guest studio overlooking a beautiful green pasture leading to a private forest with paths that led to a magical bridge and singing brook. The main house, unfortunately, was not as charming as the setting, but we summoned up all of our resources, ordered a large dumpster and began the task of gutting and renovating, a job I had sworn I would never do again. Chris and I worked at our regular jobs during the day and became construction workers at night. This went on for nearly six months. The chill of winter was a great motivator to continue until everything was sealed up and ready for the long Berkshire winter.

Miraculously, we were able to finish enough of the house to have a Christmas party. Both Chris and I think of this time of year as special and sacred. We were thrilled to have friends come and celebrate with us in our new home. I was able to take time off from work to prepare for the party, but Chris was busy at his job and he started to show the strain. Chris had struggled with a susceptibility to lung problems since childhood and I witnessed the severity of it in our first few months of dating when he was hospitalized for almost a week with pneumonia. I have since been aware that when he is over-tired he is the most susceptible to an attack. So naturally when I saw the strain in his face I became concerned. He assured me, however, that he was fine and I should not worry.

The party was a tremendous success. Everyone loved our new home and the amazing transformation that had taken place. We took before and after pictures and put a photo album together to show others, but also to remind us of what we went through in case we were ever tempted to do it again. I knew that all I had to do was open the album to the old black tile in the kitchen that was put on with a tar-like substance or the sixty years of wallpaper that had to be steamed off the walls to stop me from ever again buying an old house in need of a little tender loving care.

A breathtaking snowfall arrived right on schedule for Christmas with another one on New Years Eve. Being a New Years' baby, I got to choose how we would spend it. After all the commotion, I was happy to elect a quiet night at home and a lazy beginning to 1992. On my forty-second birthday, I was given a gift that did not appear to be a gift when I first received it but that I have come to value in retrospect. It was the gift of the seventh Obsidian Trial.

That night, Chris came to bed looking white as a sheet. I asked what was wrong and his reply cut right through to the depth of my fear. He said that his heart was acting up, that it felt like it was going to stop. He had been in his study in deep concentration just to keep his heart going. I put my head on his chest to listen to his heartbeat. When I held his wrist to take his pulse, I could barely find it. His heart was beating faintly at an eerie, erratic rate. It sent a chill up my spine. I insisted that we go to the hospital immediately, but he didn't want to move, and assured me that it would pass. For the first time, he shared that he had experienced these episodes all of his life, which he thought might be related to the heart condition that had kept his father out of the army. In spite of being a fitness buff with his love of jogging, weight lifting, and skydiving, these phantom 'heart collapse' episodes would sneak up on him about once a year, and on more than one occasion had nearly killed him. He had given up on doctors, who could never find the cause, and was more or less resolved to living with it.

I had known Chris to be one of the most intelligent people I have ever known, including anyone that I had read. I felt grateful to be married to this man that I loved and was deeply honored to share my life with such an evolved spirit. Now I saw this dream of our life together flicker like a candle as it burns down into the dish, drowning itself in the liquid wax. Could this be happening? Was the man I loved and waited so long for dying? I remembered the promise I had made to God just before meeting Chris, when I told Him all I wanted was to know real love before I died, even if it was only brief. I meant those words then, but did I mean them now? I didn't want to lose him so soon. We had only been married a few months. It was much too soon. As I watched Chris' life force flicker and dim, my fears and feelings of powerlessness surged like the sea during a hurricane.

Chris made it through that night one breath at a time. The next morning, sunshine sparkling on the newly fallen snow, gave us a ray of hope. He had stabilized, but we both knew it was by no means over. It was a temporary respite from what would become an all too familiar pattern in the next six months.

Chris had spent most of his adult life exploring every form of alternative and allopathic medicine, including herbs, tinctures, acupuncture, even standing on his head, to try to lick his "phantom" health issue. Nothing seemed to work for very long. He shared his discouraging pattern. At first, we would become hopeful with some new approach when his heart and lungs would respond for a time, allowing him to feel "normal" temporarily. But two or three months later, our hopes would be dashed when the episodes returned as frightening as ever. We spent the next few months traveling to different doctors and healers, who all helped a little, but not enough for true lasting effects. Chris would frequently ask me to work on him but I always avoided the request. I feared what I might find as well as the possibility of not being able to help him either. I guarded my hope by not facing whatever the truth might be. I was surprised that Ioch hadn't pointed out my behavior because he was usually quick to show me how the choice of denial (and it was always a choice) only led to postponing and compounding the inevitable. Only the truth and the whole truth, no matter how painful and terrifying it may seem, is the easiest and most efficient path. With our course of action clear, we set out to find a good cardiologist, acupuncturist, and physician to oversee Chris' progress.

Chris went through a battery of tests but they did not reveal the true nature of his problem. The medical profession considered his heart condition to be an anomaly. The stress tests and echocardiagrams showed that his physical heart was as "healthy as a horse," as one technician reported. In fact, it was difficult to get the medical people to take our concerns seriously. Even in his mid-forties, Chris has the look of a physically fit man in his twenties, albeit minus the hair. He continued to have these serious attacks. I knew I could not continue to feel the fear and concern I experienced about his health and stay well myself. I had to turn Chris' health and life over to God in the same way that I had done my own. In a strange way, it seemed harder to let go of Chris. I had waited a long time for him to enter my life. This illness tugged at all of my old abandonment issues.

When I was nineteen years old, my father died of a sudden heart attack while on a plane. I adored my father and still remember vividly the last time I saw him. I had come out to the house in Long Island from Manhattan to talk with him about my plan to move to California after graduation and also to resolve an old difference that was still not healed between us. He was so busy enjoying himself that we never had an opportunity to talk, and the next morning he was scheduled to fly up to Rhode Island to see my mother.

That morning we shared a quick cup of coffee as he nursed a hangover. I remember thinking to myself how old he looked. He had never appeared that way to me before. My dad was always the life of the party, the handsome, witty, story teller that everyone loved. He gulped down the last of his coffee as our neighbors pulled in the driveway and honked, indicating they were late for the airport. He grabbed his bags and rushed out the front door as I stood there, disappointed but resigned. He saw me through the dining room and came back to kiss me goodbye. As I watched him walk down the path to the car, I thought, "Why is there never any time?"

A few hours later when my sister drove me to the train station to go back to the city, I was filled with a dark chill. I knew that death was in the air. I asked my sister if she ever wondered how she was going to die, at which point she dismissed me and my morbid question. But I knew, and later it was confirmed, that at that exact moment my father was dying. There was so much unfinished between us. This was a pain that went beyond description and would haunt me for years. I swore I would not let another relationship end that way if I could help it. If things needed to be said, I would say them before it was too late.

Now, once again I asked myself, "Why is there never any time? Ioch, I prayed, I know that I need to let go, but everything in me wants to hold on even tighter. I know I can't control this situation, but every cell in me is screaming to at least try. I need you to show me the way. When I see Chris turn white as a ghost and struggle for each breath, I feel my fear ripping my heart to pieces. I know that I can only be of help if I am in the atmosphere of acceptance, but how do I accept something I fear so greatly?" I fell to my knees and waited for his reply, it came softly and gently:

"Santi, when God asked Abraham to kill his only son for Him, Abraham felt at first that the horror of the request would drive him out of his mind. Why would God want to take the son that he had waited all his life for and who had filled his life with a joy beyond description? But God did not waiver in his request, nor did He explain His reasons for such an impossible demand. After a time Abraham, aligning with his love of God, accepted God's Will and began to prepare for the sacrifice of his son, but at the very last moment God stopped him and let his son live. What is the lesson in this?"

I thought for a moment and then remembered something that Elisabeth had said when I was in Switzerland. "To find God," she said, "you must surrender the thing you love the most to Him, and in that surrender you will know God."

"Is that the meaning of this lesson, Ioch? Am I to surrender Chris to God as I have surrendered so many other things in my life that I felt I could not live without. Is that feeling of needing someone or something in order to go on simply placing that person in God's position?"

Ioch interrupted my questioning, "As in the other lessons that are layers of understanding to be peeled away, layers that leave the learner more and more exposed. It is in complete vulnerability that the final lesson is learned and true freedom experienced. This is the last of the Obsidian Trials.

"*Trial Number Seven*: <u>Surrendering all that you love, including your body and your mind, to the life and death cycles of God's creation.</u>

"Abraham agreed to God's request because he trusted the word of God because all things of God are love and therefore all requests and events loving regardless of their appearance.

Seeing beyond the appearance that the ego perceives to be the truth is the first layer to this lesson. The ego of man has created hate, fear, torture, disease and disempowerment and then conveniently placed the blame and the responsibility on God. The ego must learn to take responsibility for its creations if it is to learn how to create differently. Abraham aligned with trust and his son was spared but the lesson goes far deeper than that."

Suddenly, I began to understand. It was as if I had been putting together a giant jigsaw puzzle with thousands of pieces, I had managed to get all the similar pieces together in stacks, but the ultimate picture was still obscured.

"Ioch, I think I am beginning to understand not just this trial, but all the trials. They are like a hologram and all the pieces hold within them all the elements of the others. Abraham's trust and love for God made him willing to do the unthinkable, because in that surrender he understood that God was really asking him to do nothing. What the ego sees as an unthinkable horror, the spirit understands as nothing, merely illusion."

Genuinely pleased, Ioch asked me to elaborate and detail how the other lessons interface with the final one. Finally after fourteen years and just as predicted, I was understanding and therefore freeing myself from the hold of the Obsidian Trials. It was as if I were taking my final examination and the teacher asked the crucial question and my mind leapt for joy because it was the question I knew most about and I was assured success. Enthusiasm caused my heart to race as I proceeded to transcend the fourth lesson and see the apron of the fifth laid out before me.

"The first three trials are the trials of the ego or the personality self. Surrendering all forms of desire, want, or need to God. Success is accomplished when the self understands that all forms of denial and escape must be eliminated because in truth they are a form of reliance on darkness. Addiction is simply a symptom that the individual has placed fear in the position of God and darkness in the position of truth. Emanating from this perception come the beliefs in lack, limitation, envy and lust. Codependence is the natural result of this condition where one individual aligns with another (or an institution) as a means of illusory wholeness and safety. When we surrender in the first lesson, we surrender our worldly desires. We stop making fear our God. None of the trials can be accomplished until we recognize God as the center of our being and His benevolence as our birthright.

"*The Second Trial*: The fear of losing all your worldly possessions. This lesson, like the first, points out the misperception that loss is real and that we can protect ourselves from loss by worrying about it. Whether you are blessed with many worldly possessions or a few is not the issue here. Your relationship to ownership is the lesson. A grateful heart that recognizes God's grace and appreciates the blessings understands that we cannot lose what is rightfully ours. Anything we may have that is temporarily in our world, and thus not rightfully ours, is of no real importance. The fear of loss evaporates in light of this understanding.

"*The Third Trial*: Non-attachment to the transitory aspects of the world. Here the self wrestles with the fear of change and its resistance to the impermanent nature of the physical world. We human beings are like prisoners in a high walled prison in which all that we can recognize as our world are our fellow prisoners and the meager possessions within this darkened confinement. We struggle to squelch our feelings of powerlessness, the most dreaded emotion of the ego, in petty attempts to control our environment and those that live with us in it. This takes us on a roller coaster ride where at times we feel powerful and safe, only to be dropped into a deep well of resentment and fear around the next turn. It is only when we begin to perceive ourselves as more than human beings and open to the magnificent spiritual nature that is our true Self that we begin to rise up above the walls of the prison to view the world as God created it. When this happens, the fear of change and the desperate need to control falls away, much like the cocoon of the caterpillar as the butterfly emerges.

"The first three lessons involve the surrender of desire, loss and change which, in fact, is not a surrender at all. This is the irony I have come to understand in these lessons. There is really no such thing as surrender. The ego needs to be taken through the process of surrender because the ego desperately wants to control, but once the surrender is complete within the self, the higher Self sees there is only freedom in letting go. Now the self, having been lifted up above the prison walls to glimpse the world of the spirit, is presented with the next challenge.

"*The Fourth Trial*: <u>To be of one mind with God, free from the personal will of the ego</u>. At this juncture, the self begins to be controlled more by its spiritual nature and less by its human nature. The shift in perception can only be maintained and strengthened by the individual offering to God his or her free will as a gift of gratitude. When a human being surrenders his or her will to the Will of God, miraculous events begin to take place because the personal will is the only possession that a human being truly has, and therefore is the greatest gift that could possibly be given.

This lesson is a pivotal point in the journey. The rest of the trials are no longer based on struggling with one's ego because the ego has been brought under the watchful eye of the spirit. Now the challenges travel deeper into the core of one's soul, seeking out any darkness that has attached itself to the being at any moment in time. The ego's wounds that shut out the light of God have been healed and the soul's wounds are now brought to the surface.

"*The Fifth Trial*: <u>Surrendering all pain to God without reservation</u>. Why would anyone have reservations about surrendering pain to God? Most of us fear pain and when in pain, we make it bigger and stronger than God. When a person is engulfed in physical, emotional or spiritual pain, it appears real and powerful. When we hold on to our pain and identify with it, we make it more powerful and thus deepen our soul wounds. When we identify with darkness, we wound our soul. The challenge in this trial is to recognize that if the individual identifies with pain in any form, it is aligning with he belief that we are separate from God and therefore are subject to pain, punishment and death."

The more we fear and/or identify with pain, the more separate we feel from God which, in turn, leaves us feeling comfortless. The fifth trial asks us to recognize that we are experiencing pain but not to attach to it. Instead, we can immediately give the pain to God. This simple act allows us to feel at one with God even if the pain is not relieved. Not all pain will disappear, but it will no longer be used as a source of one's identity. Pain of any kind will simply be pain, and not a matter of who we are or what we deserve based on some feeling of inadequacy or guilt.

"*The Sixth Trial*: <u>To be fearless and forgiving in all circumstances</u>. This one I must admit took a very long time to fully understand Ioch, but I think now perhaps I do. Part of the reason why it was so hard to surrender my pain to God was that I felt it was justified by the way I had been mistreated by others. Letting go of that belief and recognizing how much I used my stories of abuse as a means of manipulation and making others feel responsible for my happiness was a difficult thing to face, but a very necessary one. I held myself hostage, blocked from the Grace of God, filling my inner house with self pity, judgment and proud superiority over those who had harmed me. I had identified with the abuse so much that I eventually could not see myself as anything else. The concept of forgiveness felt like either a burden or an ideal, but certainly not a tangible reality. It was only when I surrendered my pain and therefore my identity as having been abused that the concept of forgiveness began to shift."

As I felt more at one with my Creator, I began to feel more at one with all living things. I saw myself as part of the greatest of humankind's achievements as well as the most horrendous. I was no longer better or less than everyone. I was merely a part of everyone. Judgment thrives in the black and white thinking of the ego, but if we allow ourselves to walk down that road, it will pull us back into the walled prison. My compassion strengthened as my aloofness diminished. The process of forgiveness began as I shifted away from judgment towards simply evaluating if whatever it was that I observed was right for me. I would question whether it supported my allegiance with God or deters me from my calling. Whether a particular path was right for anyone else was not my concern, for only that individual could determine that."

"I guess you could say, Ioch, that I began to mind my own business. This afforded me a lot of free time.

"You had always instructed me to look for the jewel that was hidden in my pain. In retrospect all I see are jewels. My deepest tragedies have all contained my most powerful teachings which were the seeds for my transformation. This is best illustrated in my relationship with my mother. By far, she has been the most powerful of all my teachers because her lessons were the most difficult."

My relationship to my mother was fraught with contradiction. On the one hand, I loved her deeply and we were like-minded. We were gifted in seeing beyond the veil. We loved yoga and God and remembered past lives together. We would paint out at the light house, write plays and then act in them. In private, we would speak of the spirit world. The other side of our relationship, however, involved violent beatings when she was drunk, being humiliated regularly because of her jealousy of me and in the end, caring for her as she died a slow and painful death from acute alcoholism.

At first when she passed away, I felt relieved. But as the years went by, the bitterness left my heart and I began to feel grief and compassion. I had been given the gift of sobriety. She had not. I realized the nightmare that she lived out would have been my fate as well, had I not been freed from the obsession to drink. I could no longer feel self-righteous and judgmental towards her. That level of the lesson had been lifted. Slowly, I began to understand the true gifts she had given me. "The jewels," as you would say, Ioch. I forgave my mother for what she had done and recognized that I was fully capable of performing her deeds, especially if I continued to drink.

I thought that was the essence of the trial, but you were quick to point out that I was only scratching the surface. I was pretty discouraged at that point because I had been scratching the surface for twelve years. Then a miraculous event took place that transported me effortlessly to the true meaning of forgiveness.

Chris and I loved the Christmas season. We traveled from church to church throughout advent, getting as much out of this sacred time as possible. Christmas morning we woke early and decided to attend service offered at a local church. There were only a handful of people, but the minister was happy to give a full communion service, complete with Christmas carols. As the minister prepared for communion, Chris and I stood in prayer. Suddenly I felt a presence next to me. I opened my eyes to see what it might be, and there she was. My mother stood calmly looking at me. As our eyes met, the twenty years she had been dead melted away and here she was standing before me. After a few moments she said, "I want to move on. Will you forgive me?" At first I was startled, and then I replied, "There is nothing to forgive. Go and be happy." She smiled and my eyes filled with tears. Chris did not see my mother, nor did he hear her request. But he most surely sensed her presence and the effect it had on me. A moment later she was gone, and Chris and I went up to the altar to receive our communion.

What I understood in that moment when she asked my forgiveness was that there was nothing to forgive because all events, no matter how they appeared, were for my highest good. If we focus on finding the good in these painful lessons and not on the pain, we will come to understand. I had nothing to forgive her for because all that she gave me were jewels that led me closer to God. The essence of the Sixth Trial is that there is nothing to fear if you remember God, and there is nothing to forgive if you offer your pain to Him and are willing to accept the jewel of glory it has to offer you.

"So Ioch, forgiveness is simply seeing the true value in the trials of one's life and not being lured by appearances on the surface."

"You have learned well Santi, but the final lesson is death. Is this still something you want to control?" Ioch paused, waiting for my reply.

I was struck by the irony of the question and began to laugh. "Oh Ioch, how do you put up with me? I can be so slow at times. All the trials are within one another. If I do not understand them all, I understand none of them. My fear of Chris dying is simply a symbol that I need to surrender completely or I have not surrendered at all. I see now, Ioch. I understand desire of anything is desire of all things, fear of losing anything is fear of losing all things. Resisting any change is resisting all change. Not accepting God's will absolutely is not accepting it at all. Any pain is all pain, any fear is all fear, any lack of forgiveness is being unforgiving. Finally, not surrendering something that you love to God is not surrendering anything to God."

Humbled by this revelation, I dropped to my knees and prayed:

"Dear Heavenly Father, I have seen myself once again further along than I really am. My pride has blinded my path. I now in this moment offer it all to You, everything I fear, everything that I have felt hurt me, everything that I wanted with all my might and everything that I love. I give You my body, my mind and my spirit knowing full well that it was always Yours by right as my Creator. What am I if not Yours? Chris is not mine, my gifts are not mine and this life is not mine. How silly of me to ever think that I owned anything. I don't want to fight for little things anymore. I see now the only thing that I truly have is Your love. What more is there? Thank You for showing me the truth."

"Ioch, I feel I have gone around in circles and now I am back at the beginning. All of my efforts did not go towards building a life but simply peeled away the illusions. I stand before you stripped and simple, no more than a child of God and certainly no less. Have I completed the Obsidian Trials or am I still merely scratching the surface?"

Ioch affectionately laughed, "My dear Santi, you have in this fourteenth year completed the challenges of the Fourth Trial."

My joy and relief were immediately disturbed by a tremendous ringing in my ears and the feeling that I was moving rapidly through a tunnel, much like the sensation in the Great Pyramid. After a few moments that seemed like eternity, I realized I was in a place I had seen before in my dreams. My physical self was back home observing me here. I was, in fact, in two places at the same time. The stone forum had several rows of stone benches upon which people in white robes sat. They appeared to be witnesses or observers. In front of me were seven elderly men with beautiful silver hair and bright blue eyes. Ioch stood next to me which was so reassuring. Then one of the elders began to speak:

"Congratulations, Santi. You have completed your seven trials, and we present you with the apron of the sacred warrior. This victory demands that the candidate oversee the battle of good and evil while remaining unattached to the apparent results. If you become attached, fear and evil will grip you and the forces of darkness will have a doorway through which to enter. Your challenge is to spread light and hope in the form of these teachings. The Obsidian Trials and now the lessons of the Law of One are to be shared with anyone who is willing to learn."   "But," I interrupted. "I know very little of the lessons of the Law of One. I know that they are stored in the Secret Tenets, but I do not feel able to fully recall let alone teach of their great wisdom and scope."

The elder smiled as did Ioch and then he said, "You know more than you realize. If you trust in us, we will instruct you. The mind does not need to know what the soul has held for centuries. We are the Council and we have been teaching you in your sleep state for a very long time. If you allow yourself to remember, you will. We have been here all along, watching you every step of the way. You have now entered the next seven year period. This is the time of teaching, traveling and recording the lessons of the Law of One. People will be put in your life to help you, none of them arbitrarily. They are all old friends. With some you will connect deeply, while others will be with you only for a brief time. But they are all part of the plan. Each will be blessed and will be a blessing."

"Go now and fight the sacred battle for the kingdom of Heaven. Your sword is truth and your armor is the love of God. Like the angel Michael, be fierce in your love and nothing will defeat you."

The next thing I knew, I was back home. Ioch and the Council were gone. I felt as if all my energy had been drained. It was as if I were dying. Life seemed distant even though nothing external had changed. Was I really dying or was this the state of detachment they spoke of? I had no answers, just a deep yearning to rest. As I closed my eyes, Ioch appeared before me beaming.

"When you finish your book on the Obsidian Trials," he said, "your life will be over and a new one begun. You will be called back to Egypt for the discovery of the Secret Tenets and there you will be reunited with your blessed father, Ptahstepenu. Then, Santi, the circle will be complete and

your journey Home assured. Rest now. You have spent fourteen years clearing away misperceptions, and now we can
begin to build!"

*   *   *   *   *

A final irony.

After confronting my fear around Chris' health, the
answer to the puzzle of his mysterious heart "attacks" came
from a most unexpected source.

We walked into the Lea Tam Acupuncture Center on
Boylston Street in Boston, anxious to meet Tom Tam, a
native of China and widely respected master of acupuncture
and Oriental healing. Our appointment was late in the day,
due to the three hour drive, and there was no one in the
waiting room except for one Chinese man who was reading
a newspaper. We waited with anticipation for some time.
Suddenly the Chinese man with the newspaper jumped up and
said, "Okay, let's go!" We had been sitting next to the
unassuming master for fifteen minutes, expecting some
Chinese Wizard of Oz to appear from the back rooms.

With disarming charm and remarkable speed, Tom Tam
came up with his diagnosis of both of our health needs just by
observation and without the use of traditional pulse reading
as a guide. Beyond some metabolic and dietary recommenda-
tions, his surprising assessment of Chris' problem was a
pinched nerve in his spine behind his heart which, when
triggered by physical or emotional overload, shut down the
neural communication to his heart. A series of regular
acupuncture treatments and a closer look at the emotional
trauma that he had been holding in his heart area resulted in
a major breakthrough.

Within weeks of his first session with Tom Tam, Chris
was taking a wilderness survival course at Fort Bragg, North
Carolina, where he managed to complete the Army Ranger
Obstacle Course without a peep of complaint from his heart.

Now I am entering the next seven year period of my life. This journey has taken me far beyond what I could have possibly imagined. My old familiar self is fading into the background as the new me steps forward. "The new me" is really a strange description for someone who was there all along, observing from behind my eyes as this life has unfolded. It is the detached one waiting within each of us that has always been and always will be. It is the one who knows and remembers deep down beneath all the fears and forgetting. A veil has been taken away and a truer reality has been revealed to me. It has been worth all the pain that it has taken to come this far. I step forward embracing the path ahead, whatever it may hold.

"Seek and ye shall find...knock and the door shall be opened."

- Jesus

Epilogue

Last night I had a dream that I was back in the town of my youth. I was taking my husband Chris along the path away from school towards my family home. What was once a clear and scenic trail was now overgrown with bramble bushes and clinging vines. Even the houses along the way were covered with ivy and appeared abandoned. Each step we took became more difficult as sharp thorns and vines threatened to cut and entangle us. Our energy was being drained and the final hill loomed before us seeming incredibly large. As my tired body urged me to give up, my resolve to make it home strengthened. I became more determined to overcome these obstacles. They would not defeat me. As Chris and I made it over the crest of the hill, the path suddenly opened up to the old familiar grassy trail of my childhood. Fragrant wild flowers and bluebirds accompanied us on the final leg of our journey.

As I reflected on my dream this morning, I was struck by some similarities it had to the process of writing this book. Both processes were slow and filled with obstacles. It was ten years after my trip to Egypt before I finally felt ready to write down those experiences. Both the intensity of the experience and the inner struggle needed to subside before I could seriously sit down and begin to document all that had happened. I realized it was essential to totally accept and embrace my spiritual gifts and guides before I could share them publicly. I knew that certain people would be critical and/or skeptical of my experiences, so I needed to be firm in my resolve, regardless of how others reacted to the material.

Another struggle I had to overcome, and perhaps the greater one, was how deeply personal this material is and how exposed I would feel as a result of writing this book. Although I have a social nature, I am perhaps the happiest when I am alone.

These obstacles in my inner world were one part of the struggle, but it has been the outer sabotage that most delayed the completion of the book for so many yeas. In the five-and-a-half years it took to complete the manuscript, I had three new lap top computers burn up. The timing of each blowup is as interesting as the fact that they did. All three were destroyed while I had a deadline to meet. The first occurred just after I finished the proposal and was printing it out to send to the publisher. The second froze and then died during a month-long writing retreat on which I was to finish the manuscript. The third conked out when it was only three months old, as the final chapter was being printed for my literary agent.

One might call this bad luck or coincidence, but I suspect it is more complex than that. My agent thinks it is my energy, and she may have a point. I have a hard time with electrical devices. During the final six months of finishing the book, I destroyed two computers, three coffee pots, and a couple of answering machines. When Macy's small appliance department sees me coming, they duck. I know that as a healer I have a different energy pattern than I had before. My secretary Lois won't let me anywhere near her computer. In fact, she doesn't even like me to be in the office when she is working on the manuscript. However, I feel this may be only part of the story.

In the last eighteen years, as I struggled to overcome the seven Obsidian Trials, I have come to a better understanding of the so-called "forces of darkness." It seems that the more we move towards the light, the more these forces try to pull us back into fear, disempowerment, and defeat. I suspect that these are ultimately the product of the false ego, panicking at the prospect of being dethroned. I see now why the trials demand that we develop a 'noble warrior' within us. It is essential that we understand deep within our hearts what is worth fighting for and never let defeat be an option. I wanted to share my struggles with you to emphasize that obstacles are a part of the process and that we need to see them as problem-solving opportunities rather than omens that something is not meant to be. Don't give yourself an excuse to quit on your dreams or your inner calling.

Chris has a great expression that he heard from an old World War II fighter pilot; "If you're getting a lot of flack, you must be over the target." It was so much easier to keep going when I adopted that way of thinking. It was easier in the problem-solving department, but not in relation to my fear. The dark forces use fear as a means of control, which is why it is essential for us to shift our reliance on fear to a reliance on God. If fear is master, we will not overcome the challenges of the seven trials. The dark forces used many techniques, especially in the last year as I was nearing the book's completion, to scare me into abandoning the project. I could cite countless examples, but one in particular threatened more than the others and struck a chord of fear that had never sounded before.

I was in my bedroom writing a few pages before Chris and I were to go out to dinner. We had just returned from a nice walk on the beach with the dogs. Chris was planning to shower first while I finished up a chapter. I was deep in thought, typing away, when suddenly an unknown force grabbed my left hand and began to squeeze it so hard that my wedding ring bent, cutting into my finger. I screamed loudly and Chris came running into the room to see what was wrong. I feverishly tried to remove the ring before it broke my finger. Once Chris understood what I was trying to do, he helped me get it off. My hand was in excruciating pain after having been squeezed so tightly and my wedding ring was virtually flattened. We both stood there staring as I held it in the palm of my hand. He asked what happened, but I didn't really know. I was happily writing one minute and the next, some unseen force grabbed my hand as if to break it.

The crushed wedding ring certainly illustrated the power of the force. I was so upset that it had been my ring. I couldn't imagine how the jeweler could fix it because it looked as if it had been run over by a truck. Miraculously, the jeweler was able to return it to its original shape, looking the way it did the day we were married.

Although the ring had been repaired, I wasn't. This particular instance was the hardest one to shake because I had been personally and violently attacked by a force that I could not see or protect myself from, or so I thought.

Days went by. I was afraid to start typing again for fear something else would happen. When I was alone in the house strange things began to occur. All the fire alarms sounded and no matter what I did to shut them off, they would not stop. The sound was deafening. I finally had to call an electrician and have them all disconnected. After a few more attacks, strangely enough, instead of becoming paralyzed with fear, I started to get angry. As my anger surfaced, I could feel the warrior stirring within my belly. I became ready to take them all on.

A few hours later, I was out in the woods behind my house walking the dogs, and I began to scream at these forces of darkness: "I am finished being afraid! That's it, understand? No matter how powerful you are, you are not as powerful as God and my Circle! I call on the protection of my Guides to guard me and instruct me! You are not going to stop me! You are not going to scare me! You are not going to stall me any longer! I will not be defeated and I will not pay any more attention to you!"

I walked briskly back to the house and began to work on my manuscript. There were no more physical attacks.

As in my dream, the path cleared as I crested the hill and all my struggles simply faded as my focus turned to the wild flowers and bluebirds. I share this with my readers with the hope that if you are struggling or feeling attacked by forces that you do not understand, ask the forces of light to help and protect you. Summon up the warrior within to lead the way, and do not allow anything seen or unseen to stop you from answering your call.

God bless you, and I hope to meet some of you along the way.

References

Page 3-4: Imhoptep was chief architect of the pharaoh Zoser of the Third Dynasty who built the step pyramid at Sakkara, c2670 B.C.E.

Page 10: The Great Pyramid refers to Cheops which is located at Giza and covers 13 acres and 481 feet wide at each side of its square base. (Brad Steiger, Overlords of Atlantis and The Great Pyramid, p.100.)

Page 11: In the beginning, Horus was imagined to be a sky god whose image was seen as a falcon with outstretched wings. His eyes were regarded as the sun and the moon. (Manfred Lurker, The Gods and Symbols of Ancient Egypt, p.65.)

Page 12: Search For God, Books 1 & 2. Compiled by the study groups of the Association of Research and Enlightenment (A.R.E.), Inc., Virginia Beach, Virginia, 1942.

Page 15: "There were evidences and prophecies of Atlantis being broken up, and Egypt was chosen as one of those places where the records (the Secret Tenets) of that activity or peoples were to be established." (Edgar Cayce Readings, #275-38 F.21, 1/16/34).

The final destruction of Atlantis, which plunged the mighty civilization beneath the waves, occurred around 10,000 B.C. (Brad Steiger,

Overlords of Atlantis and The Great Pyramid, p.48.)

Page 18:   "Sons of Belial were of one group, or those that sought more then gratifying, the satisfying, the use of material things for self, <u>without</u> thought or consideration as to the sources of such nor the hardships in the experiences of others. Or, in other words, as we would term it today, they were those without a standard of morality." (<u>Edgar Cayce Readings</u>, #877-26, p.76.)

Page 28:   "Iranian situation" refers to a group of Americans who were taken hostage at the U.S. Embassy in Teheran in 1980. President Carter pressed hard in the summer and fall of 1980 to negotiate with the Ayatollah for their release. He was not able to do so before the November elections and, subsequently, lost miserably to Ronald Reagan. I was in the Middle East at the time of these negotiations.

Page 35:   Sons of God, came from the star Sirius (Sothis) to Atlantis. They brought with them a divine consciousness and knowledge of all the secrets of nature. (Earlyne Chaney, <u>Initiation in The Great Pyramid</u>, pp.43,44.)

The Children of the Law of One were souls who had taken material/physical form. Dating from the First Destruction, the population of Atlantis divided itself into two camps. Those who kept their souls pure in the physical "self" were the Children of the Law of One. The others were the Sons of Belial. (Brad Steiger, <u>Overlords of Atlantis and The Great Pyramid</u>, p.51.)

Page 36: The Firestone - Large crystal with both construc-
tive and destructive forces. Housed in a giant
domed building lined with non-conductive metals.
Akin to asbestos. (Edgar Cayce Readings, #440-5-
M.23, 12/20/33.)

Temple of Iltar housed the giant crystal
(Firestone). It will rise again. There will also be
the opening of the temple or hall of records in
Egypt. (Edgar Cayce Readings, #5750, p.308.)

Adytum, the Holy of Holies - sacred inner
chamber beneath the Sphinx where Ptahs and
pharaohs held council. (Earlyne Chaney, Initiation
in The Great Pyramid, p.43.)

Page 37: The Law of One (First Law) - the forces without,
the forces within, must coordinate. For they that
attune themselves to the divine within will find the
mental and the material taking their proper place in
material affairs. (Edgar Cayce Readings, #1003-2-
M.25, 3/6/37, p.90.)

Page 47: Knut, House of Light was the site of Egypt's secret
ceremonies of initiation into the cherished seventh
degree of the Mysteries. It is also known as the
Great Pyramid or Cheops. (Earlyne Chaney,
Initiation in The Great Pyramid, p.43.)

Page 48: Caduceus - the symbol worn on the apron of a
third degree initiate. (Earlyne Chaney, Initiation in
The Great Pyramid, p.137.)

Page 78: Endometriosis is a condition in which some of this
endometrial buildup backs up through the fallopian
tubes and into the pelvic cavity. This growth

causes problems as it spreads, creating adhesions (which can cause infertility) and pelvic pain. (Niels Lawersen, M.D., and Steven Whitney, It's Your Body: A Women's Guide to Gynecology, p.333.)

Page 83:   Self, when capitalized in this text, refers to one's higher Self or transpersonal Self. The part of us that is deathless and beyond our personality.

Page 90:   Katrina Raphaell, Crystal Enlightenment, The Transforming Properties of Crystals and Healing Stones, p.94.

Page 115:   Gary Zukav, The Dancing Wu-li Masters, p.239.

About The Author

Pamela Santi Meunier resides in her native Rhode Island. Santi is a practicing Psychotherapist and the Executive Director of Galactica Institute for Personal & Professional Development. She specializes in transformational growth and healing, as well as recovery from trauma, abuse and addiction. Since the early 1980s she has led hundreds of groups through her pioneering healing process. Santi has developed a national following with her powerful spiritual teachings and their practical application in everyday life. Santi lectures on the OBSIDIAN TRIALS, and other related subjects. You may contact her through:

Galactica Institute, 25 Hamilton Ave., Jamestown, RI 02835 (401) 423-3330 e-mail Galactca@aol.com.

If you would like to be on our mailing list, write or call us to receive a free copy of our newsletter and Santi's workshop schedule.
Abundance & Health!